STORIES FOR CHRISTMAS

Compiled by
PAUL MORTON-GEORGE

DENHOLM HOUSE PRESS
Robert Denholm House, Nutfield, Surrey RH1 4HW

This book was first published in 1973

© Denholm House Press 1973

ISBN 0 85213 073 2

Made and printed in Great Britain by
Cox & Wyman Ltd., London, Reading and Fakenham

EDITORIAL PREFACE

THIS book is intended to provide story material at Christmas time for use by teachers both in day school and on Sundays; by ministers and lay preachers in church; in week-day organizations; for parents to read or tell to their children, and in some cases for boys and girls to read themselves.

The majority of the stories have been specially written for this book, but some material has been adapted from publications now out of print, also from *Partners in Learning* and from Take Home Papers.

The age-groups for which the stories are intended are as follows:

Stories 1–7: for 3–4 years
Stories 8–11: for 4–6 years
Stories 12–18: for 5–7 years
Stories 19–27: for 6–8 years
Stories 28–36: for 7–10 years

How appropriate these divisions are will, of course, depend on local conditions, and upon the story-teller's own judgment.

If users prefer to tell a story in their own words, the age-range for which it is suitable can in a number of cases be much wider than that indicated above.

CONTENTS

Suggested key to age-groups for which the stories are suitable can be found in the Editorial Preface.

CONTRIBUTORS

	Stories		*Stories*
E. D. ABBOTT	15	PAT McINTOSH	14
MABEL AUSTIN	11, 22	WILLIAM J. MAY	20
MARGARET BACON	3 (with	PAUL MORTON-GEORGE	33,
C. Bacon), 7, 24			34, 35
STELLA BIRCHALL	9, 10	ROSEMARY RENOUF	1, 4
MARGARET CLARK	21, 27	IVY RUSSELL	16, 17, 18
K. MORGAN CRANE	6*	FRED SPRIGGS	8, 12, 36
LILIAN COX	19, 25,* 30	ROSEMARY STEPHENS	31
MARY ENTWHISTLE	29	DOROTHY I. TAYLOR	23
ERNEST H. HAYES	28	VERA E. WALKER	26
DIANA K. JONES	2, 5	ANON	13, 32

* indicates re-told by writer

I

The Blind Visitor

It was Christmas morning. Jane and Bobby had had such fun pulling their presents out of their Christmas stockings. Mummy and Daddy did like the calendar and the bookmark that Bobby had made at playschool. They were so pleased and they each gave Bobby a big hug. He had helped Jane to make a star for Mummy and Daddy, and they thought it was beautiful and they hugged Jane too.

'Now we must tidy up and get ready for church,' said Mummy. We must not forget that old Mrs. Martin is coming home with us to share our Christmas Day. 'Goodee!' shouted Jane and Bobby together. Mrs. Martin was blind and they were both very fond of her.

After the service at church, Jane held Mrs. Martin's hand and Mummy took her arm to help her walk along the road to their home. Bobby waited for Daddy. Once they were in the warm sitting-room, Mummy got some coffee for Mrs. Martin and orange juice for Jane. 'Now I must finish getting the dinner ready,' Mummy said. 'Will you look after Mrs. Martin, please, Jane?' She gave her Mummy a little hug. 'Of course I will,' she said.

First Jane drank her juice. Then she saw that Mrs. Martin's coffee cup was empty. 'Shall I put your cup on the tray?' asked Jane. 'Oh, yes, please, dear,' said the old lady. 'Then you can tell me what you had for Christmas.'

Jane got the toys one by one and gave them to Mrs. Martin, telling her about their colours. It made Mrs. Martin so happy to hear all about these things, and Jane loved to tell her.

Soon Bobby and Daddy came home. 'Do you like our Christmas tree, Mrs. Martin?' asked Bobby.

'As soon as I walked into your room,' she answered, 'I guessed there was a Christmas tree, because I could smell the leaves. It makes the room feel Christmassy. Please tell me what it looks like, Bobby.' So Bobby told Mrs. Martin about the star at the top which he had made at school; about the angel which was really Jane's tiny doll; about the coloured lights and the glittering tinsel, the coloured balls and, most of all, the beautiful golden ball where you could see your face if you looked right into it.

Jane and Bobby helped Mrs. Martin across the room so that she could touch the golden ball. 'How beautifully smooth it is,' she said slowly. 'Your face must shine and smile as it looks back at you from there. And the leaves are quite sharp, nearly like prickles where they touch my hand. Oh, how soft the tinsel feels. It really is a beautiful tree.' Jane and Bobby stood still as they watched Mrs. Martin. Then they put out their hands and felt the tree and the tinsel and sniffed. Yes, there was that Christmassy smell. They had been so excited about the bright, glittering colours and lights that they had not noticed the other lovely things about the tree.

'Dinner is ready,' said Mummy, peeping round the door.

'Have you noticed the prickly feel of our Christmas tree, Mummy?' asked Jane, as she and Bobby helped Mrs. Martin into the dining-room.

'I hadn't really thought about it,' said Mummy, 'but I know what you mean. Did Mrs. Martin help you to discover that?'

'Yes, Mummy,' said Bobby, 'And do you know that the big, golden ball is not only round and shiny, but is very, very smooth too?'

'You really have had fun finding things, without even going outside our own house!' said Daddy as they all sat down to enjoy the Christmas dinner which they had smelled as Mummy was dishing it up in the kitchen.

As Jane and Bobby were getting ready for bed after a very happy Christmas Day, Bobby said thoughtfully, 'Do you know, Mummy, I am glad that I have eyes and can see, but I am glad that Mrs. Martin has helped me to notice how things feel and smell, too.'

'Yes,' said Mummy, 'Mrs. Martin is a happy person who makes up for what she can't see by enjoying all her other senses as much as possible. In our prayers, shall we say "Thank you for our eyes"?'

'Yes,' said Bobby thoughtfully. 'And thank you for exciting things to smell and feel that we don't always notice.'

'And for a lovely Christmas, and Mrs. Martin,' joined in Jane.

2

Happy Christmas, Postman!

'MORE cards,' shouted Robert as he heard the clatter of the letter box; and he and his twin sister Helen raced one another into the hall to see what the postman had delivered. Mummy followed them and looked at the envelopes; there were two for Mummy and Daddy and one for Robert and Helen. 'A card for us; a card for us,' they sang.

One of the cards for Mummy and Daddy had a picture of a Christmas tree all bright with presents and tinsel and the other was of a lovely robin with a bright red breast who looked as if he wanted to sing and sing because it was Christmas time and he was so happy. The twins opened their envelope and laughed with delight. The card was from Auntie Jean and Uncle Bill and had a picture of a snowman with a big red scarf and a jolly grin.

Every morning after that, as soon as Robert and Helen heard the clatter of the letter box and the plop on the mat, they ran to the door singing, 'It's the postman; it's the postman.' 'More cards; more cards,' and they picked them up and took them to their mummy. What fun it was opening the envelopes and finding the pretty cards inside.

One morning, instead of a clatter at the letter-box, the postman rang the bell. The twins rushed to open the door. But when they got there, they could hardly see the postman because of the big parcel he was carrying. 'Happy Christmas,' he said as he handed the parcel to Mummy. 'Happy Christmas, postman,' laughed Robert and Helen.

They took the parcel inside and soon Mummy had untied the string and Robert and Helen helped to take off the brown paper. How exciting it was! Inside were four smaller parcels all wrapped in gay Christmas paper and tied with red bows and on each was a little note saying, 'Not to be opened until Christmas Day'. Also tied to each parcel was a little label with a tiny Father Christmas in the corner. One said, 'With love to Helen from Auntie Pat and Uncle Harry.' Another said, 'With love to Robert from Auntie Pat and Uncle Harry.' The other two parcels were for Mummy and Daddy and each had a label just like Helen's and Robert's.

It was great fun trying to guess what was inside their parcels. Robert felt his. It was a square shape. 'What could it be?' He turned it over and over but he couldn't guess what was inside. Helen's parcel was oblong. 'I wish I could have ust one tiny peep,' she said, but Mummy said 'No, that would spoil the surprise.' 'Let's put them under the Christmas tree then we can open them with our other presents on Christmas morning,' said Robert.

When they had arranged the parcels under the tree, there were more cards to open and then they went into the kitchen with Mummy. They were going to make mince-pies today! 'Christmas is fun!' said Helen as she arranged the little trays for the mince-pies.

'How many more days before Christmas?' she asked Mummy a little later, as she put a spoonful of mince into each little pastry case. 'Only one more day,' said Mummy. 'Tomorrow is called Christmas Eve and the next day is Christmas Day. Tomorrow will be the last day the postman will call with Christmas cards.'

'Oh,' said the twins, a bit disappointed. 'Do you think the postman would like to see all the cards he's brought?' asked Robert.

'That's a good idea,' said Mummy. 'We'll invite him in for a minute or two when he calls tomorrow.' 'And we can give him one of these nice mince-pies,' said Helen. 'Yes, and a cup of coffee,' said Mummy. 'That will help to keep him warm while he finishes delivering his cards.'

Then Mummy had another idea. 'Why don't you make a Christmas card to give to the postman?' she suggested. The twins thought that would be fun and they set to work. Mummy gave them lots of pictures she'd cut from last year's Christmas cards. It was fun looking through the pictures and deciding which one to choose. It must be a very special card for the postman. At last they found just what they were looking for. A picture of Jesus asleep in his mummy's arms; with the animals in the stable looking at the baby and three shepherds kneeling. Jesus' mummy was smiling and the shepherds looked very very happy.

Mummy came to see the picture they'd chosen. 'Yes,' she said, 'that's the best picture of all. Christmas is the time when we remember Jesus' birthday and that's the reason why everyone is so happy and why we send cards and presents to one another. I'm sure the postman will be pleased with his card.'

The twins carefully stuck the picture on to the plain blue card Mummy had given them, and then inside Mummy wrote in pencil, HAPPY CHRISTMAS, POSTMAN. WITH LOVE FROM HELEN AND ROBERT. Helen and Robert went over the letters with their coloured pencils to make them look gay.

How pleased the postman was when he called next day! He admired all the cards and enjoyed the mince-pie and coffee which Mummy had made. Then Robert and Helen gave him their card. He took it from the envelope, looked at the picture and smiled. Then he opened the card and looked at the words inside. 'Yes,' he said, 'Christmas is a very happy time!'

3

Men who saw the star

IN a faraway country there lived some Wise Men. They read their big books and wrote things down, and talked to each other. Sometimes they went out at night and looked up at the stars shining brightly in the sky. 'How wonderful the stars are,' they said to each other.

One night they were looking up at the stars when they saw one which had not been there before. It was much brighter than the others and shone with a lovely silver light. 'That must be a very special star,' said one Wise Man.

'Yes,' said another. 'I think it means that a great King has been born.'

'Shall we travel together to see the baby King?' asked the first Wise Man. 'Why, yes!' said his friend. 'We will take some presents with us, to give him when we get there.'

There was much to do before they could set off. They had to prepare food for the journey, and choose clothes to wear and tents to sleep in on the way. They chose some very special presents, to take with them, and wrapped them up very carefully.

When they were quite ready, they set out. They travelled in the night-time, because then they could see the bright star shining to show them the way. The lands they travelled through were very hot, so in the daytime they rested in their tents. It was a long journey and sometimes they got tired, but they kept on because they wanted to find the baby King.

After many days they came to a big town on a hill. 'There is a King's palace here,' said one. 'Perhaps that is where the baby is.' They went to the palace and asked, but no one had heard about the baby.

'I wonder where he is?' said the Wise Men, one to another. Then they looked up and saw that the star was farther away, beyond the town. 'Come along,' they said. 'That's the way, over there.' They followed the star and then they came to the little town of Bethlehem.

When they came into the narrow streets of Bethlehem they asked, 'Can anyone tell us where there is a little baby boy?' Someone took them to where Jesus was, with Mary and Joseph.

Quickly they unpacked their presents and went in to see the baby. 'A wonderful star has led us here,' they said. 'We know your little baby is going to be a great King, so we have brought him our very best presents!' They were so happy that they had found the baby King at last.

4

The Christmas Tree

JANE was so excited! She kept darting across the room to peep through the window. Bobby, her brother, should be coming home from school any time now. It was the last day of the term and Bobby had taken a carrier bag to school that morning to help him to bring all his things home. Jane wondered what he would have.

Ah! That was the click of the gate! Mummy went to open the door and Jane was right behind her. Bobby took off his coat and went straight up the stairs with his bag. Jane followed him to his bedroom. 'Look, Jane,' said Bobby proudly, 'I made this calendar for Mummy's Christmas present and this book-marker for Daddy.'

'Oh, they are pretty,' said Jane. 'I shall be glad when I can go to school too.' Bobby put them into his drawer under a book to keep them safe till Christmas Day. Then he got out some decorations.

'I like that one,' said Jane, standing still for a minute to look at the brightly painted star. 'Daddy will soon be home. He promised that we can help him to decorate the Christmas tree. Your star will look lovely on it. Can I take it downstairs to show Mummy?'

'Well, be careful and don't break it. I'm soon coming down,' answered Bobby.

Mummy looked at all Bobby's decorations and helped him to decide where they should go. The candle and holly fixed with plasticine into a foil dish looked beautiful on the window ledge. Soon Daddy came in, and he was very pleased to see the beautiful decorations Bobby had made so carefully. Then he brought the Christmas tree in from the shed. It was fixed very firmly into a tub and Mother got some newspaper and crêpe paper to stand it on.

Then Daddy got a box from the loft. Bobby dusted it carefully and Mummy opened it. There lay the glittering tinsel, the coloured balls and the lights which had been packed away last Christmas all ready for this Christmas. Bobby remembered them all, and which was his favourite coloured, shiny ball. It was larger than the others and a glorious golden colour. Jane could not remember much about last Christmas, but she found all these pretty things so exciting that she just could not stand still at all!

First, Daddy put Bobby's star at the very top of the tree. It was just the right place for it. 'It is like the star that led the Wise Men to Jesus,' said Bobby.

'Yes,' said Jane, 'And can we put an angel near the top, like the one that sang to the shepherds?'

Mummy looked in the box. 'Oh, I remember, last year the paper angel looked dirty and broken so we threw it away. We shall have to make another one.'

'Can we use my little doll?' asked Jane, already on her way upstairs to fetch it. Mummy found some tissue paper and some paper doilies and soon Jane's little doll was on the Christmas tree, the most beautiful angel Jane had ever seen.

Now the lights were working, and were fixed on the tree. Daddy was arranging some tinsel near the top. 'May we put some tinsel round the bottom of the tree, please Daddy?' asked Bobby.

'Be careful not to push the tree over,' said Daddy. 'You put some on that side, Bobby, and Jane round this side.' Then the coloured balls had to go on.

'Let's put the super gold one right in the middle,' said Bobby, and that's where it went. It was just level with his eyes, and when Bobby looked straight into it, he could see his own face looking back at him.

'I want to see, too,' said Jane, so Daddy lifted her up to look. 'Oh, oh,' was all she could say as she gazed at all the glittering colours and her own face, there in the golden ball.

'Tea is ready,' called Mummy a few minutes later. Bobby,

Jane, Daddy and Mummy sat at the table. It was Bobby's turn to say grace. 'Thank you, God, for our pretty Christmas tree and for our lovely tea, Amen,' he said.

5
Jean's Christmas Party

WHEN Mummy called for Jean after playschool she found her very excited. 'We're going to have a Christmas Party,' said Jean. 'A fancy dress party; what can I go as, Mummy.' The words came tumbling out all at once and Mummy laughed. 'That will be fun, Jean. We'll have to think very hard about what you can wear.'

All the way home, as Jean sat next to her mummy in the car, she thought and thought about what she could wear for the fancy dress party. She tried to remember all the characters in her story books; Goldilocks; Looby Loo; Cinderella; the fairy in Sleeping Beauty; Little Red Riding Hood. Yes, that was a good idea. 'Mummy, could I go to the party as Little Red Riding Hood?' she asked.

Mummy thought for a moment. 'Yes, you could wear your new blue dress and the little white apron that I had when I was a little girl, and I could make you a nice red cape and hood with the material that Grandma gave me last week.'

'Red Riding Hood had a basket, as well,' said Jean. 'I could carry the one Sandra gave me for my birthday.' Sandra was Jean's older sister. She was 8.

Jean could hardly wait for the day of the party. Every day she asked Mummy, 'Is it today?' and Mummy would say, 'No, not today.' At last the day came when Jean asked, 'Is it the party today?' and Mummy said, 'Yes, it's this afternoon.' Jean jumped up and down and clapped her hands with excitement. 'I'm going to a party; I'm going to a party,' she sang.

She hunted for her basket and filled it with the groceries which Mummy had said she could borrow. She remembered that, in her story book, Little Red Riding Hood was taking groceries to her grandmother when she met the wolf in the forest.

After lunch Jean put on her new blue dress, her Mummy's white apron and the new red cape with its hood that Mummy had made. She felt very excited as she picked up her basket and waited for Mummy to bring the car round to the front door.

When they arrived at playschool, Jean could hardly believe her eyes, the room looked so lovely. Quite different from when she had seen it last. There were paper decorations everywhere and in one corner of the room stood a big Christmas tree with decorations that glittered and shone; fairy lights; and right on the top of the tree the biggest silver star Jean had ever seen. The record player was playing 'Rudolf the Red-Nosed Reindeer' and some of the children were singing and dancing in a ring. Anne, who lived round the corner from Jean was dancing and Jean ran across to join them. Anne was dressed as a fairy and Jean thought her dress was lovely. Then she saw Paul dressed as a cowboy. He kept pointing his gun and saying 'Bang, bang,' which made everyone laugh.

When all the children had arrived, Mrs. Davies made them get into a big circle for the judging of the fancy dress. Mr. Davies had come to the party and he was going to be the judge. Jean liked Mr. Davies. He was great fun and let the children have rides on his back. Mr. Davies said it was very difficult to choose the winner, because all the costumes were very good and he thought they all deserved a prize. But at last he chose Mark. Mark had come as a spaceman. Second was Sally, who was dressed as a gipsy, and then Mr. Davies chose Jean for the third prize. She was so happy she wanted to skip all round the room. Her prize was a little doll with golden hair and blue eyes and she decided to call her Anabel.

After the fancy dress, Jean and the other children played games. First there was Oranges and Lemons. Jean loved it when the two teams pulled one another. The other team had more boys than Jean's and they easily pulled Jean's team over. They all laughed as they fell in a heap on the floor. After Oranges and Lemons, they sat in a circle for Pass the Parcel. Jean managed to take off one piece of paper but Anne took off the last piece and found the bar of chocolate inside. Next they played Musical Chairs, but Paul was so busy playing with his gun he kept marching round the wrong way. 'The other way, Paul,' Mrs. Davies kept saying, and this made the other children laugh, but Paul didn't mind.

When they'd finished playing Musical Chairs, Jean decided to have a go on the slide. She climbed to the top of the steps, then 'Whoosh', down she came. It was great fun. She had four goes on the slide until Mrs. Davies said it was time for tea and they all went into the next room. 'Ooh,' said all the children as they saw the tables laden with sandwiches and crisps, cakes and chocolate biscuits and in the corner two big jugs of orange juice. After they'd eaten as many sandwiches and crisps as they could manage, Mr. and Mrs. Davies brought in jelly and ice-cream for everyone. Jean got a red jelly and she was glad, because red was her favourite.

After tea came the really big surprise. The children were sitting quietly and listening for the bells which Mrs. Davies said they would hear. The bells were quiet at first but gradually got louder and louder until they were very loud and right outside the door. Then the door opened – and there was Father Christmas. All the children shouted 'Hurrah' and Jean shouted as loudly as she could. Father Christmas smiled and waved at all the children and sat over by the Christmas tree. He opened his sack and inside was a present for everyone. Jean got a paint box and Anne a jigsaw puzzle. When all the presents had been given out the children sang 'Rudolf the Red-Nosed Reindeer' for Father Christmas, and then it was time to go home. As she looked round, Jean saw Mummy waiting at the door. 'We've had a lovely party, Mummy,' she said as she ran across the room and she showed Mummy her presents and took her to see the Christmas tree.

As she sat next to Mummy in the car going home, Jean told her all about the party – the fancy dress and how she had won third prize; the games; the tea and best of all, Father Christmas.

But something was puzzling Jean. 'Mummy,' she said, 'it was a lovely party, but why do we have Christmas parties?' Mummy smiled. 'Do you remember your last birthday, Jean, when you were four?' 'Yes,' said Jean, 'we had a party then.' But she was still puzzled.

'Well,' said Mummy, 'Christmas is the time when we remember Jesus' birthday. Birthdays are happy times; that's why we have parties and Jesus' birthday is the happiest time of all and that's why we have Christmas parties.'

'I see,' said Jean and she sang the new song she'd learnt at playschool. It went like this:

> *Jesus baby Jesus,*
> *Mother Mary loves you,*
> *Rocks you to sleep.*

> *Jesus baby Jesus,*
> *All the children love you,*
> *Love Christmas Day.*

Jean's new song is copyright A. M. Pullen and is reproduced by permission.

6

The Little Fir Tree

ONCE there was a big forest. One day men came and planted lots of new fir trees.

Soon they began to grow 1ft. – 1½ft. – 2ft. – 2½ft. – 3ft. – a bit more every year. That is, all except one. The other trees used to tease him at first. 'Come on, Titch – you'll have to hurry if you want to catch us up!' Well, poor little Titch was only 2ft. high – all the other trees were now 5ft., 6ft. or 7ft. tall. Their branches pushed out.

'Watch out – you're squashing me!' Titch used to say. 'You'll never be any use, so what's it matter?' the taller trees said.

There was one tree which was a good 7ft. tall, just near Titch. 'They ought to get rid of you,' he said one day to Titch. Titch shook with fright, and some of his needles fell off. 'I want to grow up and be a big, high tree,' Titch sobbed. 'Be quiet,' the tall tree said, 'I can't concentrate on growing straight.' Titch was now four feet high. Tall tree was twelve feet tall.

Time passed and the trees grew and grew – that is, all except Titch. It was so dark down where he was now – he had a job to breathe. Some of his branches were twisted, where the tall tree and the others had pushed against him. 'You'll never be any use to anybody,' said the tall tree to Titch. 'Look at me. What a fine tree I am; tall – 14 feet – as straight as straight can be.'

Time went by and Titch was beginning to hope that the men would come along again, and perhaps cut off some of his twisted branches. 'I'm 15ft.,' announced the tall tree importantly one day. Titch sighed, and said nothing. Then he heard some men coming.

Why, they had stopped near his group of trees. The tall tree said, 'They probably want a tree for an important job – a tree like me – almost – no, a perfect tree.'

The men were talking. 'Yes, that one will do fine.' Then two men moved over to Titch, and began to dig Titch up! 'Stupid fellows,' said the tall tree. 'It must be me they need – "do fine", indeed – that twisted little thing!' Titch was speechless. What *were* they going to do with him?

They put Titch on a lorry, and off they went. They stopped outside a big house and fourteen girls and boys ran out to greet them. The children helped the men unload Titch. They took him inside the high house. Titch wondered what was going to happen to him – he'd never been in a house before. The girls and boys put him in a tub and then dressed him up with all kinds of things, coloured balls and tinsel – his twisted branches and his root hurt a bit.

Titch heard the children talking. It was Christmas! What wonderful things he heard and saw! He got so excited he almost jumped out of the tub. Titch found he was at a Children's Home – and how glad he was. What had the tall tree said? – '*You'll* never be any use to any one.' He wondered what the tall tree would say now if he could see him.

When Christmas was over they took Titch outside. He wondered what they were going to do with him now. He was put carefully into a hole which the boys had dug, and in time he took. He became part of the Home. In summer he watched the girls and boys play games and in the winter he was dressed up with gay coloured lights. Yes, he *was* useful – and happy too!

The story is based on the playlet, bearing the same title, by Una Norris.

7

Presents

IT was the Sunday before Christmas, and Simon's Sunday School teacher, who was called Betty, had just finished telling all the children in the Beginners' Department the story of the Wise Men, and how they brought their gifts to the baby Jesus.

'Now,' she said, 'You can all make a present for your mummies and daddies. Here are some sheets of cardboard folded in half to make big Christmas cards. On the front you can make your picture.'

Simon decided he was going to make a Christmas card about the story of the Wise Men. Betty had a big box full of things for making pictures, and he went to see what he could find in it. He found some gold paper, and Betty helped him to cut out a star shape and stick it on to his cardboard. Underneath this he stuck a square shape, to make the stable where Jesus was born. 'What shall we use to make the Wise Men?' asked Simon. 'How about making them out of pipe cleaners?' replied Betty. So, together, they made some shapes to look like the Wise Men. 'Now we must make some gifts for them to carry,' said Simon, and he went to the box again, where he found a silver milk bottle top, a gold milk bottle top and a piece of brightly-coloured sweet paper. They stuck all these things on to his cardboard. At the end of Sunday School Betty gave Simon a large paper bag to put the Christmas card in, so that Mummy and Daddy should not see it.

When he got home he carried it upstairs to his bedroom and put it carefully under his bed, to hide it away until Christmas Day. Simon felt very pleased that he had made such a splendid present for Mummy and Daddy, and he looked forward to giving it to them on Christmas morning.

Meanwhile, Mummy and Daddy were preparing a present to give to Simon; but, instead of hiding it under their

bed, where he might see it or hear it, they had to think of
another idea. Next door to them lived Mrs. Evans. So, when
they had bought Simon's present, Daddy and Mummy went
round to see her. 'We want to keep this present very secret,'
they said. 'We don't want Simon to see it, or hear it, before
Christmas Day. We can't wrap paper round it until the last
minute, so we can't keep it secret that way. Will you please
look after it for us until Christmas Morning? Then we will
come in and fetch it and wrap the Christmas paper round it.'
Mrs. Evans was delighted, and said she would take great
care of it until Christmas Day.

Simon woke early on Christmas morning. He wriggled
down his bed with his toes to see whether Father Christmas
had been. Yes – he could feel something heavy with his toes.
It was his stocking lying at the foot of the bed, and it was
certainly full of presents. Then he heard Mummy calling
him, and knew that as they were awake, he could take his
stocking into their room, and sit between them in their bed
to open all the exciting parcels that Father Christmas had
brought him. There was a parcel sticking out of the top of the
stocking, and when Simon opened it he found it was a toy
trumpet. He blew it several times to make sure that it worked!
Then he unwrapped the other parcels. There was a ball, a
matchbox toy car, some marbles, a little teddy bear, some
crayons, a drawing book, a packet of balloons, some
Smarties and, right in the toe of the stocking, an orange and a
ten pence piece. What a lovely Christmas stocking, and what
an exciting start to such a happy day!

When Simon was dressed he took the big Christmas card
which he had made at Sunday School from its safe hiding
place under his bed, and carried it downstairs to put it on the
breakfast table for Daddy and Mummy.

Then Daddy called him into the kitchen to help him cook
the breakfast. While they were busy, Mummy went next
door to fetch their present for Simon. She thanked Mrs. Evans
very much for looking after it for them, and carried it back,
wrapped in a big piece of gay Christmas paper, and put it on

the breakfast table just as Simon was carrying in the toast, and Daddy was following with the coffee.

Simon was surprised to see such a large parcel on the table just where he was going to sit, and was very excited by the look of it. He wondered even more when he thought he heard a faint sound coming from it. Whatever could it be? Perhaps he had not really heard anything; but no – there it was again, a strange scratching sound. Simon's eyes grew larger, and he went quite pink with excitement.

'Go on, open it,' said Mummy, 'but gently.' So Simon began to move the Christmas paper wrappings, and do you know what he found? A beautiful blue and white cage, and from inside, two bright eyes of a little hamster looked out at him. It was the sweetest little hamster he had ever seen. It had brown silky fur over its back, and white fur over its chest and tummy. When it saw Simon it sat up on its hind legs and twitched its whiskers.

'Oh thank you, Mummy and Daddy,' cried Simon. 'I shall call him "Holly" because it's Christmas.' 'That's a good name,' said Mummy, 'and it will remind us of when he came to live with us.'

Daddy and Mummy then opened Simon's present to them, the lovely Christmas card that he had made. They were very pleased with it, and thanked Simon with a big kiss from each of them.

After breakfast it was time to get ready for church, and they remembered that last Sunday their Minister had asked them to bring their favourite present to church with them on Christmas morning. 'Can I take Holly?' asked Simon. 'Well, he seems to be asleep at the moment,' replied Daddy, 'but I'm sure you could take him in his cage.'

'I think our favourite present is Simon's Christmas card,' said Mummy, 'so we shall take that with us too.'

8

'Thank You'

TIMOTHY and Jane were twins. Every Sunday they went to church with their mother and father. Mr. Jackson, the Minister of the church, was their friend and often they would chat with him. Timothy and Jane belonged to the Primary Department where they did lots of interesting things. When they finished they were eager to meet their parents coming out of church and tell them what they had been doing. During their dinner they would all talk about their time in church.

Church was always specially exciting when they got near to Christmas. A large Christmas tree was placed in the church and then at one of the services the lights would be switched on. There would be carols to sing, a special Gift Service and then best of all, the Family Service on Christmas Day itself.

Several Sundays before Christmas the teacher in their Department told the children they were going to prepare for Christmas. They were going to decorate their room. They were going to make little gifts for some lonely old people. They were also going to think of as many words as they could to describe Christmas and for each word they would light a candle. So that they knew what she meant she gave them an example, 'Christmas is a time for parties'. When Timothy and Jane told Mummy, she suggested that if they kept their ears and eyes open they would find other words.

The very next day as they went to school, they noticed the shops were full of specially wrapped gifts. They were talking about what they were going to buy for Mummy and Daddy. 'Christmas is a time of giving and receiving presents,' whispered Timothy to Jane.

The Post Office van went by with a huge notice on the side, 'Post Early for Christmas'. 'Christmas is a time for sending cards,' said Jane.

At school they were shown how to make decorations and someone brought in a Christmas tree. Each child was asked to bring a candle to put in a special holder near the tree.

When they got home, Timothy and Jane wrote down the words they had thought of during the day. 'Christmas is a time of Giving and Receiving; sending Cards; Decorations.'

One day, when they came out of school, Mummy met the twins and said they were going on the train to visit their Granny who was not very well. The train left in about ten minutes so they would have to hurry. They got to the station and within a few minutes the train drew in. A carriage door opened just near to where they were standing and as other people got out, Timothy, Jane and Mummy got in.

In the compartment was another lady and a little girl. It wasn't long before they realized that little Elizabeth was blind. She kept asking her Mummy a lot of questions and she had a strange looking book which she was reading. There were no words in it, only a lot of dots which Elizabeth felt with her fingers. Before long Timothy, Jane and Elizabeth were chatting away. They told her all about school and their church and she told them about the Special School where she learnt to read the dots with her fingers and to write with a machine which made dots on the paper.

'Come on, here's our station,' said Mummy, so they had to say Goodbye to Elizabeth and wished her a Happy Christmas. But they couldn't stop talking about her. They wondered what it was like to be blind and they told Granny all about Elizabeth. Mummy made some tea and soon it was time to return home.

When they got home Timothy and Jane played at being blind. They each had a blindfold on and they tried to find their way about. It was quite fun, except that they couldn't find their toys. Jane dropped her hair slide and had to crawl about the floor trying to feel for it. She bumped her head against a table and nearly cried.

After a few minutes they decided to remove their blindfolds and they both said together, 'I'm thankful that I can see.' 'Yes,' said Mummy, 'there are a lot of things we ought to be thankful for and Christmas ought to make us even more thankful.'

Timothy and Jane looked at each other as if they had a secret.

Next Sunday their Teacher asked if any of the children had any words to describe Christmas. 'Parties,' said one. 'Presents,' said another. 'Decorations,' said yet another. The candles were lit and they all began to realize what a wonderful time Christmas is. Then Timothy and Jane said, 'Christmas is a special time of Thankfulness.' Teacher lit another candle and in the prayer thanked God for all his gifts, especially for Jesus, the Light of the World.

9
Jenny's Story

CHRISTMAS morning. The loveliest time of all the year.

I've been looking forward to it for weeks, and now it is really here.

I'm Jenny and I'm seven.

Our house is so full that Mummy says we could do with elastic walls.

Grannie is here and Auntie Jessie with my cousins Jill and Alan. They are twins and are eight years old. They came yesterday morning and Jill and Alan and I all went with Daddy to collect our Christmas tree from the farm.

It is a huge one and now it is standing in the window all covered with silver stars and coloured balls. There are presents on it too and we are going to take them off when we have our party this afternoon.

Adam came last night with his mummy and daddy (friends of ours). He was so sleepy that he was put straight to bed so I haven't seen him yet. He is only five.

It is very early and nobody is awake but me. I'm sleeping on the sofa downstairs because Jill and Alan have my room.

I've just had a feel at my stocking and it's all fat and bulging, with lots of hard corners. I can feel a ten-pence piece in the toe.

It's not *my* sock really, but a long thick one of Grannie's. I'm longing to see what is in it but I've promised Mummy to wait until the clock strikes seven before switching on the light.

Mummy! Mummy! Look what I've found in my stocking! A tiny doll's chair, a pink hair-ribbon, chocolate mice and a balloon to blow up. It's shaped like a pig.

Oh, here's Adam! Shush! What a noise! Please Mummy tell him to stop blowing that awful squeaker.

Jill has a doll's cup and saucer and a skipping-rope and Alan has a – oh ADAM! He's at it again!

Yes, yes! I know I should be eating my breakfast but I don't feel a bit hungry. It's getting late and we have to be at the hospital soon.

Do all the poor sick children know we're going? I want to take my new teddy-bear to show them – and my scooter – and Adam wants to take his panda.

Oh, can't we take them? Then I don't want to go at all, and Adam's going to cry.

There's Daddy all ready to go. He has all kinds of toys in the car for the sick children.

Come on, Adam! And Jill and Alan. We *DO* want to go, don't we?

Ooh! What a big hospital! Long, long slippery floors and lots of very clean, smiling nurses. Ever so many little white beds with boys and girls all looking excited.

Paper streamers and holly, a lighted tree and babies with bandages on their heads, legs and arms. Some are black babies, some are brown and others are white like me and they all look very pleased to see us.

Oh look, Adam! There's Santa Claus in a red coat and a cotton wool beard, and he's started to give out the toys.

That little boy has been given a big woolly ball. That's the one I help Mummy to make last Saturday. And there's a wooden horse like the one Daddy made for Adam. And that's the doll Grannie sent.

'Away in a manger – no crib for a bed ...' Oh dear! Adam has run off.

'The cattle are lowing, the Baby awakes ...' I wonder where he can have gone.

Now we have sung our three carols and the children are waving Goodbye.

Daddy – we can't go home without Adam. Oh, that nice young nurse is looking for him. I think I shall be a nurse when I grow up.

Good! She has found him.

Adam! You didn't!!! He has been into the room where

all the old ladies are in bed and he says he has been singing 'Jingle Bells' to them.

Nobody seems to be cross with him because no one ever is cross on Christmas Day. It is the birthday of that very special baby – Jesus. I wish we could have been in Bethlehem on that night when he was born long, long ago.

That is what carols are all about, you know.

Now we are at home again for dinner. We have crackers and paper hats. Grannie *does* look funny in hers.

We four children are going to rest upstairs with our new books before the time comes for our tea-party.

Oh – I must have fallen asleep because I've hardly seen one picture in my book and it's time for the party already.

We are all dressing up and pretending to be somebody else. I'm Old Mother Hubbard with Grannie's scarf and a long dress of Mummy's and a funny old bonnet from the attic.

I've helped Adam to be a shepherd, like the ones who went to see baby Jesus. He is wearing white towels with Daddy's walking stick for a crook and a toy lamb under his arm.

Jill is an angel in some old net curtains and feathers for wings. Alan makes a fine pirate in rubber boots and a striped scarf round his head and his middle.

All the grown-ups are clapping us.

Now we are going to dance round the tree and sing 'Jingle Bells' whilst Daddy takes down the presents. Grannie has hers first. It is a pretty brooch and she is so pleased that tears are running down under her glasses.

I have a wee black doll with fuzzy hair. Adam and Alan have coloured rubber balls and Jill has a spotted cow for her farmyard.

Everybody is showing presents and there is such a hulla-balloo that nobody can hear what anybody else is saying.

Ah! It is time for tea. That's good. We are having jelly and ice-cream although it is cold outside. There's a huge log fire inside, so its all cosy and warm.

After tea we're going to play games and then roast chestnuts on the logs at bedtime. Mummy says we children can come down in our pyjamas and Daddy will tell us a story while the chestnuts are roasting.

How I wish boys and girls from all over the world could join in our Christmas Day!

Thank you, Father God, for giving it to us.

The Village Concert

DING dong! Ding dong! The bell rang out loudly in the country lane.

'Hurry, Ivor! We shall be late for school.'

Gwen took hold of her young brother's hand and together they ran to catch up with their friends.

The children lived in a Welsh village. They did not need a school bus because they were used to taking short cuts across the fields and over stiles on their way to school.

It would soon be Christmas and Gwen and her friends had gathered branches of red-gold rose hips and shiny holly to take to decorate the classroom.

Ivor was very excited. He was only five and as he climbed over the last stile he tumbled headlong over a sheepdog pup which got in his way.

'Oh dear!' cried Gwen, 'now you've left your boot behind and Ben has run away with it. I didn't know he was following us.'

The children laughed to see the shaggy Ben racing back across the field carrying the red rubber boot.

Poor Ivor didn't laugh. He hopped about on one foot shouting: 'Ben, Ben! Come back! Naughty dog!'

By the time Gwen and her friend Margaret had retrieved the boot and scolded Ben the school bell had stopped ringing.

Miss Roberts, the teacher, was not very cross because she was so pleased with the greenery the children had brought.

They decorated the classroom and practised singing carols for the rest of the morning.

It was only a small school and was near the village post office. At lunchtime the children all walked to the church hall for dinner. Afterwards they called at the post office shop for sweets.

It sold almost everything: shoe polish, Christmas crackers, fish fingers, ice lollies, books, pens and dolls.

It looked particularly gay that day. Mr. Jones, the postmaster, had just put a lighted Christmas tree in the window.

All the children crowded round outside to watch the coloured balls and tinsel being put on by Mrs. Jones who looked after the shop.

When they told their teacher that afternoon she said 'Shall we ask Mr. and Mrs. Jones to come to our carol concert?'

'Oh yes! Yes!' they all agreed.

'The concert will be about the story of Christmas,' explained Miss Roberts. 'Gwen, will you tell us what you know about it?'

'The Baby Jesus was born in a stable,' said Gwen. 'His bed was a manger. That is where hay is put to feed cattle – cows and oxen.'

'That's right,' said Miss Roberts. 'Oxen are still used in some countries to pull carts and ploughs.'

'What a funny sort of bed for a baby,' said John. He was ten, like Gwen and Margaret, and was quite clever at his lessons.

'It was the only cradle or crib they could find for him,' said the teacher.

'You see, the town of Bethlehem was crowded with people for a special occasion and there was no room in the inn. Mary and Joseph and their donkey were so tired that they were thankful to rest anywhere after their long journey.'

'I know who were the first people to see the new baby,' said John. 'They were the shepherds who saw the big shining star over the stable and . . .'

'Yes,' interrupted his friend David, 'the angels up in the sky told them when they were watching their sheep in the fields late at night.'

'Oh,' sighed Gwen, 'How I wish we could have heard those holy angels singing and have seen that glorious star!'

'I want to be an angel in the concert,' cried out Ivor.

'So do I! So do I!' joined in the other little ones.

'And so you shall, if you learn to sing all the carols,' promised Miss Roberts.

'After the shepherds had gone away,' she said, 'three wise men came from countries many miles away. They had followed the wondrous star to Bethlehem and found Jesus in the stable.'

'And they brought precious gifts and worshipped the baby boy,' said Margaret.

'I can see you know all about the Christmas story,' said Miss Roberts, 'so the concert should be a great success.'

And it *was* a great success.

The parents of all the children were there, also Mr. and Mrs. Jones from the post office, and aunts and uncles, and Gwen's and Ivor's 'Nain' and 'Taid'. That is what Welsh children call their grandparents.

The big final item was the crib scene. Even the farm animals were included in this. The naughty puppy 'Ben' was there alongside a donkey belonging to David's father.

A big brown cow was allowed to look through the window at the back of the stage. She suddenly gave a great MOO-OO and made Ivor jump. He fell against the piano and bent his angel's wings, but it didn't stop his going on singing. He took his wings off and held them under his arm. This made one little girl giggle, but the audience didn't seem to notice.

The big boys and girls were shepherds and wise men, except for David, who was Joseph, and Gwen, who was Mary.

In the crib was a doll lent by Mrs. Jones to take the part of the baby Jesus asleep on the hay.

Just before the end a group of very small children came on dressed in costumes of many countries. Two little Indian boys held up a banner on which was written: *JESUS, THE LIGHT OF ALL THE WORLD*.

Everyone joined in singing the last carol, 'Silent Night', before returning home across the moonlit fields.

'I like being an angel,' whispered Ivor to his sister Gwen as they trudged along beside their Nain and Taid.

'Woof, Woof!' barked Ben, which meant that he had enjoyed *his* part in the concert too.

Note: 'Nain' and 'Taid' are pronounced 'Nine' and 'Tide'.

II

A New Baby

JOAN lived with her mother and father in a flat in a busy town. She often wished she had someone to play with in the flat, but there was no one who lived on her floor the same age as she was. It was fun when Mummy had time to take Joan to the park to play with other boys and girls, and sometimes she had a friend to tea, but most of the time she was alone with her mother. On Sunday she went to church and enjoyed doing things with the other children. If only Sunday was every day!

One day Mummy told Joan some good news. They were going to have a baby; it might be a boy or a girl, but Joan thought either would be fun. Now there was a lot to do. When Mummy and Joan went shopping they often bought wool, and Mummy let Joan choose the colour sometimes. When they got home Joan watched her mother knit vests, cardigans, bootees and other things for the new baby and, when they were finished, Joan was allowed to put them away safely in a special drawer. The drawer soon began to get full of clothes, towels and other things the baby would need.

Daddy helped too. He got the steps and climbed up to a big cupboard in Joan's bedroom, and got down the carry-cot and baby bath which had been put there after Joan grew too big for them. Joan helped Mummy wash the carry-cot. 'I think you are big enough to dry it yourself,' said Mummy to Joan when they had washed it clean. Joan rubbed hard until it was really dry. They washed the bath, too, and then Daddy painted the outside to make it really bright. There seemed such a lot to get ready for the new baby.

One Sunday Joan came running to Mummy after church. 'Can you guess what our story was about today? It was about getting ready for a new baby!' And Joan began to tell Mummy the story. 'Mary was the mother's name,' she said, 'and she had a lot to do to get ready, just like us. She had to spin the wool to make the baby clothes, and Joseph had to make the cradle to put the baby in.' 'They were just as busy as we have been,' said Mummy.

During the next week Mummy told Joan that they were going to stay with Granny for a little while. Granny lived in a big house a long way from the town. 'Daddy will take us in the car on Friday,' said Mummy. 'What about the new baby?' asked Joan, and her mother said that was why they were going, as Granny would be able to help. 'We must get all the things we shall want for baby packed ready for Daddy to take us on Friday.'

Joan helped Mummy pack the case with some of the baby clothes from the special drawer, and they got the carry-cot blankets and baby bath ready too. Joan helped pack some of her own clothes as well, and in her own special case she put her own toys. Joan liked staying with Granny as she had her own room, and in the cupboard were toys her own mother had played with. When Daddy came home from work on Friday everything was soon packed in the car, and off they went to stay with Granny.

It was late when they arrived, and Joan was fast asleep, so Daddy carried her upstairs and she was soon undressed and in bed. Next morning when Joan woke up she thought about the journey they had made, and then remembered the story she had heard at church. When Mummy came in to get Joan up, Joan looked sad. 'I shall not be able to hear the rest of the story about Mary's baby,' she said. 'I expect you will,' said Mummy. 'Wait and see.' Joan helped Mummy put baby's things away in a drawer in Granny's house, and she was so busy that she forgot all about the story.

Next morning was Sunday and Joan went to church with Daddy and Granny. Granny took her to be with the other girls and boys, and she was soon telling them about her journey in the car to Granny's. 'We have a story about a journey,' said the teacher. It is about Mary and Joseph who you heard about last week.' 'I know they were getting ready for a baby,' said Joan. 'Yes, that is right, and they had to go on a journey like you, Joan.' Then she told them the story. Joan rushed in to Mummy when she got back and began to tell the story of Mary and Joseph going on a journey and taking the baby clothes she had prepared. 'It was just like us, but they had a donkey and could not find anywhere to stay; only a stable. But we had a car and came to stay with Granny,' she said.

A few days later Daddy came in to wake Joan up. 'Come quietly,' he said, 'and see your new baby brother.' Joan tip-toed into her mother's room, and there in the carry-cot by her mother was a very new baby. He was so small with tiny fingers and a very little face peeping out from the shawl he was wrapped in. Joan went in often during the day to look at him. Sometimes his eyes were open but more often he was asleep. She watched the nurse bath him, and saw his tiny feet and toes, and one day she sat on the bed by Mummy and held him tightly in her arms. She hoped he would grow up soon so that he could play with her, but in the meantime she could help Mummy look after him.

On Sunday she went to church and told them the news about her new baby brother, and – do you know? – she heard the rest of the story about Mary and Joseph and their new baby, born in a stable, and put in a manger for his cot.

When she got home she told Mummy the end of the story. 'It was just like us,' she said.

The Innkeeper's Son

REUBEN's father and mother kept a Guest House in a seaside town. They came to live there from another country, so Reuben found things rather strange but gradually he was learning about the customs and ways of the people in their new country.

He loved going to school. The teachers and the other children were so friendly and helped him all they could, even though he made lots of mistakes. After school he would run home to see if there were any new guests. Sometimes, there would be little jobs for him to do. He might help to carry cases up to their rooms, or tell them how to get to the Post Offices and the shops. If there were children staying he would take them to the nearby Park or down to the beach, and play with them.

There were times when people came very late at night to ask if a room were available. Sometimes he heard his father say, 'I'm very sorry, but there is no more room. Every room is full.' The people would go away looking very sad.

When Christmas came Reuben heard for the first time the story of Mary and Joseph who had to travel from Nazareth to Bethlehem and could not find a room anywhere to stay. One of the Innkeepers suggested they could sleep in the stable at the back and there baby Jesus was born. They had to use a manger for a cradle.

The children in Reuben's class at school painted pictures of the stable and the manger, Joseph and Mary, the Inn. They made lots of decorations for their classroom; cards to send to their friends. It was all very exciting. Then one day the teacher told the children that their parents and friends were being invited to the school and their class had been chosen to make up and act a Christmas Play.

They talked about it and children were chosen to be Mary,

Joseph, the Innkeeper, the Shepherds and the Wise Men. Then the teacher said: 'We want Reuben to be the Innkeeper's little boy.' Reuben was thrilled. He couldn't wait to get home to tell his parents. All evening he was thinking about it and imagining what might have happened if he had been there when Jesus was born. So he fell asleep.

'Come on, Reuben,' said a voice, which he recognized as his father's, but when he saw him, he was dressed differently – just like the people in the pictures which the teacher had shown them when they were getting the Christmas Play ready. 'I want you to give me a hand. People are crowding into Bethlehem and they all want rooms,' said his father.

'What do you want me to do?' asked Reuben. 'I want you to go into the stable and make sure that the donkeys and oxen are safely tied up in their stalls. Then you can see that there is plenty of fresh straw on the floor. A man and his wife are going to sleep there for the night because we have no room in the house. Make them as comfortable as you can and look after them in the morning.'

Reuben made his way to the stable. He was soon busy making everything as tidy as possible. While he was working, the lady and gentleman came into the stable. He felt so sorry for the lady. She looked so tired. She spoke to Reuben and thanked him for what he had done. She sank down into the straw and then said, 'Could you put some nice clean straw into that little crib, please?' Reuben thought it strange but did as he was asked. The crib was the one he used for the little baby animals. 'Could you also bring it near me?' asked the lady. 'Good night, Reuben,' she added, 'and thank you for everything.' 'Good night,' he replied, 'I'll see you in the morning.'

Reuben was awake early the next morning. He quickly dressed and taking a blanket from his own bed he made his way to the stable. Very gently, he knocked on the door. 'Come in,' came the man's voice. The lady was still lying in the straw and there in the little crib was a tiny baby. Reuben was surprised.

'Come and see our Jesus,' said the lady. 'We will always be so grateful to your father and you for your kindness and help. Perhaps when our baby is older you will meet him again. He is going to be a very wonderful person and will help a great many people.'

Reuben knelt by the side of the crib and put the little blanket over the baby. He then went back into the house to get their breakfast.

Suddenly he heard his father's voice again. 'Come on, Reuben, time to get up. Breakfast is ready and then off you go to school.' He rubbed his eyes; 'I've had such a wonderful dream,' he said.

When he got to school he told his teacher about his dream. She thought it would make a lovely scene in the play. Reuben acted his part as if it was all real. When the parents saw the play they all said, 'It was wonderful.'

13
How Christmas came to an Indian Village

IT was Christmas Eve in a village of India, but not a single boy or girl seemed to know it. There wasn't a sign of a decoration anywhere, nor any nice smell of Christmas cooking in the little houses. As for the boys and girls, they played about the dusty street and round the big pool where their mothers filled the water-jars, just as on any ordinary kind of day. Nobody seemed to have a secret or to be much pleased; there wasn't an excited boy or girl anywhere.

You see, they did not know that it was Christmas Eve. In that village no boy or girl had ever heard the story of the wonderful Babe who came one starry night long ago, and who had a manger for a cradle. No one knew about the worshipping shepherds and the Wise Men who brought presents for the baby King. So the boys and girls went to bed just as if it was an ordinary sort of night, while here at home you were as full of the loveliest Christmas secrets as you could hold, and so excited that you thought you never, never would get to sleep.

But, although the children in that village in India knew nothing about it when they went to bed, Christmas *had* come to the village. There had been a wedding in one of the little houses at the very end of the village street a little while before. The man who lived there had brought his bride from a town some miles away. Her name was Siromani and she was as lovely as her name. She had soon made friends with the boys and girls and knew them each one and where they lived. In her own home she had often told stories to the boys and girls who lived near her, and she just longed to tell the same stories to these village children. Most of all she wanted them to know about Jesus, who loved boys and girls everywhere.

On this Christmas Eve Siromani was feeling very lonely. For one thing her husband was away, and for another she was wishing she could spend Christmas with her friends in the town.

'It won't be like Christmas a bit,' she sighed. 'Nobody in this place even knows about Christmas. There won't be any carols or presents or visits or anything.'

Then suddenly a lovely thought came to her – 'If nobody knows about Christmas, perhaps I could tell them. If no boy or girl has ever had a happy Christmas, then they shall have one tomorrow.' What an exciting thought it was!

Siromani planned at once what she would do. She hurried off to the little store and bought a kind of butter called ghee. She got sugar, too, and a fine coconut. Then she hurried back and lighted her fire and put on her biggest cooking pan. Soon afterwards the men going home from their work smelled the nicest kind of smell as they went by Siromani's home. 'Mmmm, my!' they said to one another. 'Something good!'

In between the cooking and the stirring Siromani made the prettiest little paper bags and boxes that any child ever saw. Some of her wedding treasures had been wrapped in soft, gay paper. This was splendid for sweet bags, and so were the scraps of gold and silver foil she had carefully saved.

When the buttery, sugary, nutty sweets were cooked and cooled, Siromani packed some neatly into each bag, and tied them with gold tinsel. She counted her bags carefully, saying, 'Let me see. There are two boys in that home, and a girl in the next one, and in that one there are two and a baby.' So she went on until she had got ready a little present of home-made sweets for every boy and girl in the village. It took a long, long time, and even then she hadn't quite finished.

Next she piled the bags and boxes on to her biggest brass tray, opened her door and went out into the night.

Above her shone the bright stars, and a silver moon peeped from among the clouds and showed the Christmas messenger the way. When she came to the first house the door was shut. She knocked gently upon it.

'Who is there?' called someone from inside.

'Christmas is here!' laughed Siromani.

The mother of the home opened the door and peeped out. Siromani gave her the gay parcels saying, 'Here are three Christmas gifts. Give them to the children in the morning. Happy Christmas!'

Off she went to the next house. Knock, knock! 'Happy Christmas! Give these to the children in the morning.' Then to the next home. Knock, knock! 'Happy Christmas! It is the day when we remember the baby Jesus,' she told the mothers. 'It is a happy day. Here are Christmas gifts for the children, that they may be happy too.'

When all the bags of sweets had been given, Siromani knew that every boy and girl in the village had a surprise waiting for them on Christmas morning. Then she went home. 'It will be a lovely Christmas after all,' she said as she went to bed.

On Christmas morning all the happy children came to thank Siromani for the lovely sticky sweets she had made for them. 'But what is Christmas?' they asked. 'Tell us all about happy Christmas.'

So on that Christmas morning those Indian boys and girls sat listening to the wonderful story. They heard how Jesus came, a tiny baby, long ago in Bethlehem and how he is the friend of all children everywhere.

And that was the first Christmas they had ever known. But after that Christmas came every year to those boys and girls, just as it comes to us.

14

Hanna learns about Christmas

HANNA sat on the ground, leaning against the wall of the hut. She was cold, yet she chose to be outside the hut. Inside it was dark, uncomfortable and not much warmer.

Hanna was also hungry. She couldn't remember a time when she hadn't been hungry. Long ago, her mother had said, they all used to have enough to eat. Hanna thought it must have been wonderful.

Sometimes her mother told her about the farm-house they used to live in and all the animals they had. Hanna was born there, but when she was still a baby there had been soldiers fighting in the fields. For fear of coming to harm, they had had to leave the farm.

Much the same happened to many others and now Hanna's family lived with other homeless people in a village of huts.

'Quickly, Hanna,' her mother called. 'Come and get your food bowl. The other children are starting to line up.'

So Hanna ran and joined her friends as they waited for the food which was given to them every day. Sometimes they would see the lorries come to the village, unload the food and drive off again. Where they came from Hanna did not know. She was only glad that they did come.

'It's the smiling lady today,' said one of the children.

'Good,' said Hanna. 'I like her.'

She did not like all those who came to give out the food. Some seemed too busy to take much notice of the children. Others got impatient and tried to make them hurry up. No doubt, thought Hanna, they are all good people, or they would not come at all. But she liked the one with the ready smile best.

Soon the rumour came back down the line: 'The lady is giving us extra today.' Everybody got very excited. 'And a toy, too,' said someone else.

A toy! Hanna could hardly remember when she last had a toy, it was so long ago. All the children wondered what was so special about that day. Then one of the girls said,

'The lady says it's Christmas.'

Christmas. What was that? Hanna wondered. Just then she saw one of the other girls carrying a doll. Hanna had never had such a thing in all her life. How she hoped there would be a doll for her!

And there was! More exciting even then the extra food was the doll which the smiling lady put in her arms. It was the most beautiful thing Hanna had ever seen.

'Happy Christmas,' said the smiling lady. Hanna smiled back and then plucked up her courage and asked,

'Please, what *is* Christmas?'

'When I have finished serving the meal, I will tell you,' said the lady.

So Hanna and her friends sat on the ground and listened to the story of the first Christmas, when Joseph and Mary came to Bethlehem and a baby boy was born.

'And when the baby Jesus grew up, he went about helping people,' finished the lady.

'Just like you help us,' said Hanna.

And, once again, the lady smiled.

15

The Outside Christmas Tree

RUTH and Graham were going to live in a new house. They were very excited when Mother told them this and wanted to know all sorts of things about it. 'Will it be bigger than this house? Has it a garden? Where is it?' and so on.

Mother told them that they could go and see it that very same afternoon, and they went. Before Mother had even found the key to look inside the empty house, the children were exploring the garden. And there, growing beside the front door, was a real Christmas tree!

They told Mother about it. 'We can use it next Christmas. We won't need to buy one!' said Ruth.

It was a very exciting time, moving into the new house, and the children forgot all about the tree until the weather turned cold and winter came, and they started to plan for Christmas. 'Daddy,' they said, 'can you dig up our Christmas tree so that we can have it indoors and then put it back again afterwards?' 'I don't know,' said Daddy. 'Wait until Saturday and I will have a look at it.'

On Saturday, Daddy asked his friend Mr. Chester, who knew all about trees, to come and tell them what he thought. When he had gone, Daddy came in and said, 'I'm sorry, children, but Mr. Chester says if we dig up the Christmas tree it will probably die.'

'Oh dear!' said the children, 'we did so want it inside.' 'Well,' said Mother, 'if we can't bring the tree in, couldn't you decorate it where it is, outside?'

'Could we, Mother?' asked Ruth.

'I don't see why the plastic decorations like those lambs and angels shouldn't be all right outside,' she replied, 'and the little plastic bells will ring every time the wind blows!'

So, ten days before Christmas, they trimmed the tree with

all the decorations that were suitable, icicles, lambs and angels, bells and stars.

Ruth and Graham watched through the window and were glad to see that the neighbours seemed to like the tree, and when the baker called he said, 'Thank you for cheering me up on my round. I call that a real Christmas spirit!'

Presently the children noticed a very old man standing by the gate and gazing at the tree. 'Can we ask him to come in and see it?' said Ruth. Mother agreed, so Ruth ran down and opened the gate. 'Do come in and look at our tree if you like,' she said.

The old man came in. 'I call that very pretty,' he said. 'It reminds me of one we used to have outside my chapel years ago.' Then he told Mother that he was now living at the Old People's Home near by. 'We shall probably have a tree indoors, but I shall think about yours,' he said.

When he had gone, Ruth had an idea. 'Mummy, why couldn't we decorate a tree for the Old People's Home?' she asked.

'We'll see what Daddy thinks,' said Mother.

So when Daddy came home from work the children were waiting for him with their new idea. 'Can we, Daddy? We'll pay for the decorations from our money-boxes,' they said.

'Well,' said Daddy, 'I must say that your little tree quite cheered me up as I came home tired tonight. I could hear the little bells from right down the road. I'll ring up Matron at the Home and see what we can arrange.'

And so it was decided that Matron would get a Christmas tree planted at the door of the Home (Daddy was paying for it) and Ruth and Graham were to go next day and decorate it.

When the tree was planted, Ruth and Graham were there, watching. So were many of the old people who lived at the Home, only they kept in the warm and looked out through the windows. They smiled and waved to Ruth and Graham.

As soon as the tree was in place, the two children got to work, bringing out the various decorations from a cardboard box they had brought them in.

There was a light breeze – enough to make the little bell tinkle away, sounding gay and Christmassy.

When Christmas Day came and the church bells began to peal, Ruth and Graham thought of the little bells on the Old People's Home tree, and how they too would make their own happy sound. And as they listened to the bells on their own Christmas tree, they were glad they had decided to keep it *outside*!

From 'Pull of the Wind' by E. D. Abbott (Religious Education Press), reproduced by permission.

16

What can we share?

JUDY was very excited. Her teacher had just told the class,

'We are going to do a Nativity play in school this year, and some of you will be able to take part.'

Then she explained that a Nativity Play was a kind of story about the birthday of little Lord Jesus.

'I shall want one girl to be Mary,' said Miss Smith. 'She will hold a baby doll in her arms. I shall want one boy to take the part of Joseph, and other boys and girls can be shepherds and angels.'

Of course, all the little girls wanted to play the part of Mary, but Miss Smith said she didn't know yet whom she would choose.

Judy and her best friend Carol walked home together, talking about the play.

'I hope Miss Smith chooses me,' said Judy. 'I'd like to be a lady with a baby in my arms.'

'So would I,' sighed Carol. 'I hope she chooses me!'

When Judy told her mother about the play, Mummy said, 'Well, you can't all be Mary, darling! Perhaps Miss Smith will think Carol is better for the part. But don't worry – I will make you a nice dress to wear, even if you are a shepherd or an angel.'

But this didn't satisfy Judy! She wanted to be Mary, more than anything else in the world.

Lying in bed that night she remembered her mother saying, 'Perhaps Miss Smith will think Carol is better for the part,' and she put her head under the bed-clothes to try to shut out the words. She didn't want Carol to be chosen! She began to feel so jealous that she didn't even want Carol for a best friend any more.

So when she started out for school in the morning, and saw

Carol walking along just ahead, she didn't run up to her with a smile as she usually did.

Carol seemed to have changed, too. She hurried along to school all by herself. And when they reached their classroom, both little girls rushed up to Miss Smith to try and be the first one to speak to her.

'Please Miss Smith, may I be Mary?' Judy begged. 'Mummy says she will make me a lovely dress to wear if I am chosen!'

'No, let me be Mary, please!' cried Carol. 'Mummy says I can have my new baby doll to carry if I am chosen!'

Then the two little girls looked at each other crossly.

'You're horrid, Carol!' said Judy. 'I asked first.'

'I don't like you any more, Judy,' said Carol. 'I want to be Mary!'

Miss Smith stood looking from one to the other. Then she shook her head sadly, and said,

'Judy and Carol, you won't do at all for the part of Mary – not either of you! Mary was kind and gentle, that was why God chose her to be the mother of Jesus. She didn't say unkind things to her friends, I'm sure!'

Then Judy and Carol felt very ashamed.

'I have decided to give Sally the part,' said Miss Smith, 'because Sally hasn't asked for anything for herself.'

The two girls stood looking down at the floor, feeling very sad.

'Sally hasn't got a mother,' went on Miss Smith, gently. 'You two little girls have a very kind mother, so you mustn't be jealous of Sally. Just remember all the good things that God has given you – your parents, your home and your friends. Then it won't seem so bad if you have to give up one little thing for somebody else.'

That afternoon, Judy and Carol walked home together again. They had forgotten their quarrel, and were glad to be best friends again.

'It must be horrid, not having a Mummy,' said Judy. 'I think we ought to share something with Sally, don't you?'

Carol nodded.

'Yes, I think so too. What shall we share?'

Neither of them could think of anything for the moment, so they walked along holding hands and thinking. Then Judy said,

'I could ask my Mummy to make her a pretty dress for the part of Mary. The one she was going to make for me.'

'What a lovely idea!' said Carol. 'And I'll ask Mummy if I may lend her my best baby doll to carry.'

Judy squeezed her hand.

'I'm glad you're my best friend, Carol,' she said.

When the Nativity Play was put on a few weeks later, in front of all the mothers and fathers, everybody said it was the best they had seen for a long time. Sally looked very sweet in a blue and white dress made specially for her by Judy's mother, carrying in her arms a big baby doll, lent specially by Carol.

Judy was a shepherd and wore a long stripy gown, and Carol was an angel with wings on her shoulders, and it was quite obvious that they were enjoying every minute of it, even though they hadn't got the leading part. They were still the best of friends, and that was all that mattered.

17

Benjy's Pillow

A LONG time ago, in a land far over the sea, there lived a little boy called Benjy. Benjy's father was a shepherd, and he didn't get very much money for his work; so Benjy's mother often found it hard to keep her children properly fed and clothed.

One day Benjy's father came home looking very excited. He told his family,

'A wonderful thing happened last night! I was minding the sheep on the hill with the other men, when suddenly a bright light shone out of the sky. We were afraid at first, because we didn't know what was happening. Then we heard a voice speaking to us.'

'What did the voice say, Father?' asked Benjy eagerly.

'It told us to go to Bethlehem to see a little baby that had just been born. The voice said that this baby was someone very special – Jesus Christ the Lord!'

Benjy's mother gave a gasp of surprise.

'Did you see the baby?' she asked.

'Yes,' said the shepherd. 'And you'll be very surprised when I tell you where we found him. He was lying in a manger, in a stable behind the inn! Just fancy, the Lord Jesus lying on a bed of straw, just like one of us!'

'Could I go and see the baby, Mother?' asked Benjy. But his mother said it wasn't polite for everybody to go staring at the baby, especially if they didn't go with a present for him.

'If I had a present, could I go?' asked Benjy. And his mother said yes – but there wasn't any chance of that happening, for she had no money to give him to buy presents.

All day long Benjy thought about the baby lying in a manger, and at last he had an idea. The baby's head might be uncomfortable, lying on the prickly straw. If Benjy could take him a soft pillow, that would make the manger much more comfortable.

'And where will you get a soft pillow?' asked his mother sadly.

Benjy told her that out in the fields there were many prickly bushes, and sometimes when the sheep passed close to them, little bits of wool from their fleece caught on to the prickles.

'If I go round and gather up all the bits of wool, I might get enough to make a nice soft pillow,' said Benjy.

His mother thought this was a good idea, so she gave him a cloth bag to collect the wool in, and Benjy set off.

But the bits of wool on the bushes were very small, and he spent several weeks going round the fields and over the hills collecting them together. He had to walk many miles, and his hands were often torn with prickles; but at last he had enough wool to fill his bag. Then off he went to find the inn at Bethlehem.

Now, Benjy was only a little boy, and although he thought he knew the way, it wasn't long before he was lost. On and on he went, with nothing to eat but some fruit that his mother had given him. Then, trudging over a hill, he came upon a small wooden hut with a little girl sitting outside it.

She was holding something in her hands, and as Benjy passed, he saw it was a baby bird that was cheeping unhappily. He stopped.

'What is the matter with your little bird?' he asked.

'The poor little thing has lost its mother,' said the girl. 'I am trying to look after it, but it needs a soft nest to lie in. I have nothing soft to make a nest with.'

Benjy didn't really want to give away any of his precious wool, but as he listened to the poor little bird he felt he really must do something to help.

'Take this,' he said, and he drew out a handful of wool and laid it on the ground between two stones. The girl set the baby bird gently down among the wool, and immediately the frightened cheeping stopped.

'Oh, thank you!' said the little girl. 'May God reward you for your kindness!'

Benjy went on his way. The ground was rough and his feet were very tired. Presently he saw an old man coming up the slope leading a camel. The camel had a heavy pack on its back, and just as they drew near to Benjy the camel stopped and would not go on.

'Come along, come along!' pleaded the old man. 'We must get home before dark, and we still have many miles to go.' But still the camel would not move.

Then Benjy noticed something. One corner of the pack was rubbing against the camel's side, making a nasty sore place. If only there was some soft padding underneath, the poor beast would not find it so painful.

Poor Benjy didn't really want to give away any more of his wool, but he couldn't bear to see the camel suffer.

'Perhaps I can help you,' he said, and he took out a handful of soft wool and put it gently under the corner of the pack. Immediately the camel lifted its head and began to go forward again.

'Thank you, little master!' said the old man. 'May God reward you for your kindness!'

Benjy started off again. The sun was sinking and it was beginning to grow shadowy, and still he hadn't found Bethlehem. He was beginning to feel very sad.

Just then he came to a road, and coming along the road he saw a donkey, with a man walking beside it. Riding on the donkey was a woman with a cloak drawn around her. Benjy sat down on a rock and waited for them to pass.

But just as they reached Benjy the man stopped the donkey and said to his wife,

'I am worried about you, for I know it isn't comfortable to ride on a donkey for hours at a time. But it is many miles to Egypt – too far for you to walk. If only I had a soft cushion for you to sit on, things would not be so bad.'

'Don't worry. I shall be all right,' she answered, and her voice was so weary and so patient that Benjy felt he would have done anything in the world to help her. But what could he do . . . except to give the rest of his precious wool?

No, he couldn't do that – he couldn't!

'Come, let us go on again,' said the woman. And suddenly Benjy couldn't bear it any longer. He rose, and held out the bag.

'Please take this,' he said. 'It will make a nice soft seat for you.'

'What is it?' asked the woman.

'It is a bag of wool,' said Benjy. 'I was going to take it to Bethlehem, to give to the baby Jesus for a pillow. But I've already given away half of it, and now I'm lost and I shall never find him. So perhaps he won't mind if I give it to you instead.'

But there was a mist of tears in front of his eyes, because he had walked so far and worked so hard, and it was all for nothing.

Then the lady got down from the donkey, and she smiled at Benjy. It was the loveliest smile he had ever seen.

'You have found the baby you were looking for,' she said, and she drew back the cloak to show him the child in her arms. Benjy just looked and looked, and all the tiredness seemed to leave him as he realized that he was gazing at the Lord Jesus.

'We are going to Egypt to escape from our enemies,' said the mother. 'Thanks to your kindness, our journey will be much more comfortable now.'

Then the man put the cushion of wool on the donkey's back, and helped his wife to mount again.

'Goodbye!' she said. 'We shall all meet again one day.'

Then the holy family rode on towards the south, and Benjy ran all the way home to tell his parents of the wonderful thing that had happened.

18

Not Really a Witch!

TIM and Susie were playing in the front garden when Miss Wilkins moved in to the empty house next door. They stopped playing at once, and stared at the big yellow removal van. It was so big, it seemed to block the whole road.

Then three men in overalls jumped down from the driver's cabin. They walked round to the back of the van, unlocked the doors and let down the flap. Tim and Susie were so interested that they went out on to the pavement and sat on the low wall to watch.

After that the men started to unload the van. They lifted out chairs and tables, and carried them carefully into the house next door. All the furniture was big and old, and looked very heavy.

'Look at that funny cupboard, Susie!' whispered Tim, pointing. 'It isn't the same shape as our cupboards. It comes to a point at the back, as if . . .'

He stopped, as a lady came out of the next door garden and walked up to them. She was tall and thin, and she had a very unfriendly face.

'Don't you know it's rude to stare?' she snapped. 'Go away, both of you!'

Tim and Susie were so startled that they jumped up and ran quickly back to their own house.

'What a grumpy lady!' said Tim. 'I don't like her, do you?'

'No,' said Susie. 'She looks cross, like a witch!'

After that they were careful to keep out of Miss Wilkin's way.

The weeks went by, until it was the last school day before the Christmas holidays.

'I ought to go and meet Tim,' said Mummy. 'But I'm expecting a parcel to arrive. Would you stay here and wait for my parcel, Susie?'

'Yes, Mummy,' said Susie. 'I'll wait in the front garden.'

So Mummy went off to meet Tim, while Susie waited. It was very quiet once Mummy had turned the corner, and Susie wondered what to do to pass the time. She tried running round the garden path to see how fast she could go, and then she decided to walk along the top of the wall.

But there were some wet leaves sticking to the bottom of Susie's shoes, and she was just balancing along the wall between their house and the next one, when suddenly . . .

Her feet slipped, and she fell flat on her face on the stone path in Miss Wilkins' garden!

Just for a moment Susie lay there, making little gasping noises. Then she managed to get up, but oh dear! her poor knee was all grazed and bleeding. Susie stood there, and the tears began to trickle down her face.

'Have you hurt yourself?' asked a voice, and there coming towards her was Miss Wilkins! Susie was so frightened, she began to cry harder than ever.

'There, there! Don't cry, dear. Come indoors, and let me wash it clean,' said Miss Wilkins, and her voice sounded quite kind.

They went into the house with all the funny, old-fashioned furniture, and Miss Wilkins gently bathed the poor knee with warm water, and put a bandage round it. Then she wiped away Susie's tears, and gave her a chocolate biscuit to make her feel better.

Gradually, as the pain in her knee grew less, Susie stopped being frightened. Miss Wilkins had such gentle hands, and even her voice was quite different from the sharp tone she had used on the day she moved in.

Miss Wilkins was watching her with a shy little smile.

'You mustn't be afraid of me,' she said. 'I do like children . . . only I've never really known any children to speak to, so I hardly know what to say to them.'

When Mummy and Tim came back, Susie was standing at the gate waiting to tell them all about it.

'Miss Wilkins isn't a witch, Tim! She's quite nice really.

She gave me a chocolate biscuit, and she says she does like children, only she doesn't know what to say to them.'

'I hope you said Thank-you for the biscuit, Susie,' said her mother.

Susie nodded hard. She was thinking about poor Miss Wilkins, living in that quiet house all by herself.

'Yes, I did say Thank-you, Mummy. But I'd like to do something else as well. Shall I buy her a Christmas present?'

But Mummy was thinking, too. She guessed that Miss Wilkins was lonely, and now she knew that she was shy as well. That was why she never seemed very friendly.

'I have a better idea,' she said. 'Christmas is a time for making people happy; so just to show how grateful we are for Miss Wilkins' kindness today, let's ask her to come in and spend Christmas Day with us!'

Which is just what they did. And it proved to be a very happy day indeed for all of them, but most of all, for lonely Miss Wilkins.

19

The Present with a Difference

ONE wintry afternoon over two hundred years ago, a little girl sat stitching at her sampler. Outside, a wild wind raced through the bare trees, and whipped the branches till those nearest the grey stone house brushed the windows. The little sound they made startled the girl; she looked up, dropping her sewing and ran to the window. Perhaps as she stared out at the December storm she thought of bare moors where the rain slashed over the brown heather, drenching the fugitives who hid in the glens of Scotland from King George's men, loyal even in defeat to Bonnie Prince Charlie. For that was the year 1745, and even the daughter of a respected Lancashire doctor must have felt a touch of excitement.

Unwillingly enough, Dolly returned to her cross-stitch.

'Sit up, Miss Dolly,' said the stern voice of her old nurse. Dolly braced up her drooping shoulders; she was a lanky child, taking after her father.

'May I not stop now?' she said plaintively. ' 'Tis barely light enough to see, in any case.'

The old nurse took the sampler to the window and examined it closely. 'Not amiss,' she admitted. 'Yet you will have to bestir yourself, child, if it is to be ready for your good aunt this Christmas-tide.'

'I don't like sewing,' said Dolly sadly. 'Everybody sews – every girl, that is to say. I wish something different could happen to me. I wish . . . Oh, there's father!' An entirely different note rang in the last three words, and she turned to greet Dr. Byrom with a face aglow with love. The curtsey she gave him would have looked strange to us in a daughter nowadays. But it was quite natural to her.

For all that, fathers and daughters were much the same in the eighteenth century as in these modern times, and very soon, big girl though she was, Dolly was perched on the arm of the chair where Doctor Byrom's lanky length stretched before the log fire.

'You are tall, father!' she teased.

'They'll have to make a horse to fit me, my dear,' Dr. Byrom replied solemnly. 'I give you my word of honour, I've searched the shire for one high enough, and on the best I tried my legs were a-drag behind me!'

They laughed together at his comical plight. Yet, tease him as she did, Dolly was very proud of her tall, clever father, who wrote for the *Spectator* magazine, and had great men like Mr. Wesley and Mr. William Law for his friends. She only wished that she, like him, could go over the sea to France and learn to be a doctor, and come back and be famous as he was. But of course such things were not for young ladies; they had to stay at home and stitch samplers for their aunts' Christmas presents.

Dolly spoke, not for the first time, of this to her father. 'Take Christmas, for example,' she said. 'I must needs work a sampler for Aunt Emily; and she will give me a thimble, and Aunt Esther will give me perhaps a hussif; and you will mayhap give me a phial of sweet lavender water, or some such ladylike thing!' The disgust in his young daughter's voice amused Dr. Byrom, but he understood and loved her too well to laugh.

'Well, my Dolly,' he said, 'I know now that whatever my Christmas gift to you must be, it must not be lavender water! I promise I will give my daughter something quite different from any other present she has ever had or ever will have; something of which there is not a second in the whole wide world; something that shall be hers, and hers alone!'

'Oh, Father,' said Dolly breathlessly. 'What is it? Do tell me! I know Aunt Emily considers books to be unladylike; but could it be a book?'

Dr. Byrom shook his head. 'Not exactly a book,' he said tantalizingly, 'and not exactly not a book!' He reached for his wide low-crowned hat and his crooked stick and went out, leaving a puzzled and excited daughter behind.

The next Sunday Dolly went with her father to service at the chapel of Chetham's Hospital, which was not a hospital for sick people, but a big school for boys. Dolly always enjoyed service here; it seemed much more interesting than in the small, dark parish church, particularly when the boys sang one of the hymns her father had written specially for them. 'I'd rather write hymns for the lads than be Poet Laureate,' he used to say.

'I wish you'd write a hymn for me,' she suggested to Dr. Byrom on the way home.

He looked at her sharply but merely answered, 'Why, what would you do with a hymn, daughter?'

'I'd know what to do with it,' insisted Dolly. 'Will you Father, some time?'

'Perhaps, perhaps,' said Dr. Byrom and then talked about something else.

Christmas Eve came. The sampler was finished and duly wrapped and labelled. The comfortable stone house at Kersall Cell was full of cookery smells, of puddings and spices and mince pies. Dolly was late to bed and woke early next morning through sheer excitement. Yet her father was astir before her, going downstairs to put something by his daughter's plate. He stood by the fire, and watched her come running downstairs.

'Merry Christmas, Father dear!' She dropped her curtsey and then kissed him. Then she turned to the table.

'My present! The present that is to be different, and special and . . .' She caught sight of the square white paper, broke the wafer that sealed it, and opened a sheet written in her father's careful hand.

' "Christmas Day – For Dolly",' she read from its heading, then glanced down the page.

'Father! Is it really for me? It's a new hymn, a Christmas hymn. It's a Christmas carol! Oh Father, have you really made it for me, all for me?'

They read it together, taller father looking over tall daughter's shoulder.

Christians, awake! Salute the happy morn
Whereon the Saviour of mankind was born;
Rise to adore the mystery of love
Which host of angels chanted from above. ....

and so through the dignified, stately verses that yet pulsed with the Christmas joy, that is the most wonderful joy of all. Dolly's voice grew breathless with excitement; it was her father who read the last verse:

O may we keep and ponder in our mind
God's wondrous love in saving lost mankind;
Trace we the Babe who has redeemed our loss. ....

and so the end.

'Father, how ever can I thank you?' said Dolly. 'It's the best Christmas present a girl ever had.'

Other people soon came to agree with Dolly. It was always specially 'her' carol, but the next year, 1746, Mr. Harrop published it in his *Manchester Mercury*; and Dolly was more than a little thrilled to see it in print. Mr. Wainwright, the organist of Manchester Parish Church, made a special note of it; and from his brain and pen came the tune we know and sing.

A year later, when Christmas-time approached, he had a happy thought. He taught his choristers both hymn and tune, and on Christmas Eve the party of them journeyed out to Kersall Cell. They stood in the frosty starlight, and when John Wainwright gave the signal the boys' voices, clear and true, rang out in that lilting carol of joy:

Christians, awake! Salute the happy morn
Whereon the Saviour of mankind was born ...

Dolly within the house listened with special pride. 'My carol!' she said.

c

20

The Shepherd Who Stayed Awake

'LITTLE Brown-face,' said Nimrod the shepherd tenderly, 'it hurts me that you should suffer so.' The quick, short breathing and the occasional little cries of pain were pulling at the shepherd's heart. She had been a delicate lamb, and Nimrod had had great trouble to rear her at all.

Tonight even the nest Nimrod had made did not seem to comfort her. He wrapped his great cloak about her then laid the sheep gently down near the fire. The other shepherds were inclined to laugh at him for the trouble he took.

But one night, when they had been laughing at him, old Samuel had silenced them by saying, 'A merciful man is kind to his beast. God will be kind to those who have been kind to the works of his hands.'

'Does God take thought for sheep?' Black Dan had inquired in his rough fashion.

'Some say,' Aaron had answered, 'that God does not take thought even for shepherds. We cannot leave our flocks to attend the services, and we are too poor to offer many sacrifices, and Rabbi Jeshua says that a shepherd is little better than a publican, for are not they accursed who do not keep the Law?'

'I think sometimes,' old Samuel answered in his thin quiet voice, 'that the good God is better than men's thoughts of him.'

Black Dan prepared to roll himself in his cloak and lie down to sleep, then cleared his throat.

'If God cared about us, he would be near,' he muttered; 'he would come to our help.'

The others made no reply. They felt that the conversation had drifted on to dangerous ground. The Rabbis would put a man out of the synagogue for saying as much as that.

One by one the shepherds wrapped themselves in their cloaks and lay down to sleep. Only Nimrod lay awake. The sick sheep coughed restlessly and now and then moaned a little. Nimrod talked quietly as though to help her by his company. What Black Dan had said stayed in his mind.

'If God cared about us, he would come. If God cared.'

Nimrod looked at the little houses of Bethlehem, white in the moonlight, and thought about all the people under those flat roofs.

'If God cared – he would come.'

He got up and stood looking round the fold at the huddled masses of the sheep. He would risk his life to find one of those sheep if it were lost. He would sit and watch by one who was sick, as he was doing now. Surely the good God cared about men as much as he himself cared about sheep.

'If God cared – he would come.'

Strange that Black Dan should say a thing like that – Dan who seldom went to the temple and was always saying hard things about rabbis and priests, who never cared about religion. Strange . . .

Suddenly there was a great blaze of light, as though the sun had risen in a flash. The other shepherds sprang to their feet with cries of alarm. The sheep roused up and stared bewildered. The dogs whimpered. It was something they could not understand. There was a sound like a rush of wings, a vision as though an angel clothed with light had suddenly come to them. Dazzled and frightened, the shepherds flung their cloaks across their faces and threw themselves upon the ground.

'Fear not,' – the voice was like the notes of a silver trumpet – 'behold, I bring you good tidings of great joy which shall be to all people. For unto you is born this day in the city of David a Saviour which is Christ the Lord. And this shall be the sign unto you. You shall find the babe wrapped in swaddling clothes, lying in a manger.'

The voice gave them confidence and assurance. They looked up to listen. There came singing whose beauty was greater than anything they had ever dreamed.

'Glory to God in the highest and on earth peace, goodwill towards men.' At last the light began to fade, the strains of the music grew fainter; then it ceased entirely.

The dogs came rubbing against their masters' legs as though they needed some assurance. Nimrod stopped and patted a shaggy head. He, too, needed something to tell him that he was in touch with things he could understand. If God had chosen to come, he would have come to those who were familiar with his ways, to those who waited in his temple, and kept his Law, not to shepherds abiding in the fields keeping watch over their flock by night.

'Come, let us go to Bethlehem.' It was Black Dan who spoke, shaking himself as though he were fresh roused from sleep.

Up the hill they went in silence to the little sleeping town. The things they had seen and heard that night were not such things as men could talk of easily. The narrow, twisting streets were deserted. They came at last to where a lantern hung before the wide gateway of the old, square inn.

Their loud knocking brought old David, the porter, to the wicket gate, rubbing sleepy eyes and grumbling loudly as he came and fumbled with the bolts of the door.

Black Dan broke in upon the old porter's mumbling.

'Is it here that the baby has been born of whom the angels have been singing to us?'

'And do you think that I have time to concern myself with babies?' exclaimed the porter. 'Here we have the inn so full of folk, if I had ten pairs of legs and twenty hands I could not have answered half the calls that have come this night.' The old man stood there at the gate with the lantern swaying to and fro in his hands while the stream of his complaining ran on and on as though it would never end.

Nimrod stretched out a hand and laid it on old David's shoulder and shook him gently. 'Come, come, David. Where have you been this night that you have not seen the sky ablaze with light and heard the singing in the sky?'

'Been? Where I should have been? With the inn all full of folk, what time have I had to watch the heavens? And all the time more people coming and more . . .'

The old man was well started again, but once more Nimrod pulled him up. 'Where is the child who is born in Bethlehem this night? The child of whom the angels have been singing?'

'Child? child? There is but one child in the inn. But he is not a child of whom any angels will sing. His father is a young carpenter, who has been living in Nazareth, and came with his young wife riding upon a donkey, and at first I turned them away as I turned away so many others. But the woman looked so weary that I let them have the place we use for a stable. And a boy was born two hours and more ago.'

The shepherds hurried across to the entrance to the stable that belonged to the inn. They lifted the heavy sheet of tent cloth that hung before the entrance and peered in. A swinging lantern helped them to see a little group against the farther wall. There was a bearded man in early middle life whose kindly faced looked glad, yet more than a little anxious, too. Lying on a roughly-made bed of straw on the ground was a young woman. In a tall manger a little child lay asleep.

They tiptoed clumsily across the uneven earthen floor, and stood for a moment looking at the sleeping child. Then something about him, or something of the memory of the things they had seen and heard that night, made them kneel.

It was long before they found their tongues, but at last the shepherds told the story of the light and the music and, most amazing of all, the messages that were so far beyond their understanding.

'Black Dan had been saying that if God cared, he would come. And the angels say that he *has* come, 'wrapped in swaddling clothes and lying in a manger,' just as we have found him. And no one heard the music and no one saw the

light except us poor shepherds. So it must be that the good
God takes thought for shepherds, after all.'

They took their leave and passed out one by one. Then the
tent cloth lifted again and Nimrod returned. He fumbled in
his great brown shepherd's coat and pulled out the soft white
fleece of a lamb.

'A gift for the baby,' he said.

Then he raised his hand in reverent farewell and went out.
Little Brown-face might be needing him again.

21

St. Francis' Crib

ONE December morning, over seven hundred years ago, two
men stood among the trees on the lower slopes of a range of
hills north of Rome. One of the men was in the rich clothing
of an Italian nobleman. The other wore the rough brown
robes of a monk, and his feet were bare. He was pointing to
the rocky crags above.

'Look, Giovanni,' he said, 'the cave is there, just above
that cleft in the rocks.'

'Yes, Francis, I know the place you mean.' Giovanni da
Vellita was Lord of Greccio, and the wealthy owner of all
the land in this area. He was a great friend of Francis, the
poor saint of Assisi, and was always ready to do anything he
could to help him. Now he listened intently as Francis told
him about his plans.

'I am very troubled,' said Francis, 'because people seem to
have forgotten why we celebrate Christmas. They don't
really understand what it means, and they don't enjoy
Christmas as they should. I want people to realize just what it
was that God did for us, and how poor he chose to become for
our sakes.'

'Jesus wasn't born in a palace,' Francis went on; 'he was
born in a stable very like that cave up there on the hillside.'

'Now, Giovanni, this is what I want you to do. Make a
figure of the Babe of Bethlehem. Then build a manger in that
cave, and fill it with straw and hay. And on Christmas Eve I
want you to send along an ox and an ass to stand on either
side of the manger. At midnight we will invite everyone to a
Christmas service there. If people can see with their own
eyes what it was like when Jesus was born in Bethlehem,
perhaps it will help them to understand.'

Giovanni became just as enthusiastic as Francis about the
plan for the Christmas service. He arranged for a carpenter

to build a manger against the back wall of the cave, and had it filled with hay. An ox and an ass were borrowed from a farmer, and on Christmas Eve they were led up the steep slope from the village of Greccio to the cave on the hillside.

Meanwhile, all the people in the surrounding villages had been invited to attend the midnight service. The night was cool and still on Christmas Eve and, as darkness fell, a few stars could be seen twinkling in the sky. Soon the hillside was aglow with the torches and candles of men, women and children coming from all directions towards the cave high up among the rocks. The little processions of villagers were singing as they walked, but when they neared the cave all became quiet. They had been told there would be a surprise, but they had never expected it would be like this!

'Look there's a light in the cave,' said a little boy. 'I can see a baby asleep on the hay in a manger,' said his sister. 'There's an ox and an ass there, too,' pointed out their mother.

It was just as if the scene in Bethlehem had come to life in their own land, within a few miles of their own village home!

There on the hillside, looking towards the scene in the stable, they held their midnight service of prayer and praise, and Francis told the story of the first Christmas. He reminded them of the long journey made by Mary and Joseph from Nazareth, and of their arrival in Bethlehem only to find there was no room for them in the inn. Francis went on to tell them how at last they found shelter in a stable with the animals, and how Mary had to use the manger as a cot for the baby when he was born that night.

Most of the people who came to the service that Christmas Eve lived in poor little stone cottages in the villages round Greccio. For the first time they realized that when Jesus was born in Bethlehem he must have experienced much more discomfort and poverty than they did themselves.

'God chose to be poor for our sakes,' they said. 'He understands all our hardships. He cares for us. How wonderful it is to know that he loves us so much.'

For the people of Greccio, this was the happiest Christmas they had ever known.

22

Friends in Need

JOHN sat watching his favourite television programme. It was getting near Christmas and he was hoping they might show some things he could make for presents, but up to now it had been a boring talk, and John was not paying much attention. Then he looked up and saw a picture of an old lady huddled by a small fire in a very small room. He listened to the old lady talking to her visitor.

'I get dinner three times a week from meals on wheels,' she said, 'and a neighbour gets my pension and my shopping once a week, but otherwise I am alone!' The picture on the television switched back to the studio and John heard the interviewer ask the question.

'What are we going to do about people like this? If we could buy a coach and take the people to a centre during the week they would have people to talk to and would not be lonely,' she said. 'This costs money so we are asking you to send us old paperback books and we can sell them, and with the money buy a coach.' John quickly called to Mummy to take the address down, and when his father came raced to meet him and asked for any old paperback books he had.

When John went to church on Sunday he joined in news time. 'I saw a programme on television about old people who were lonely, and how if we collect enough paperback books we can buy a coach to take them out,' he told Miss Green, his teacher, 'and I have already found some and sent them in the post.'

'Maybe we could help too,' said Miss Green, 'but I wonder if we could do something for some old people in our town. What do you think we could do?'

John and the other children began to think. 'It will soon be Christmas,' said John; 'could we give them a present?' 'Yes,' said Miss Green, 'but they would still be lonely.' 'I know,' said Mary, 'we could invite them to come here and we could give them the presents then.'

John and the others thought that was a good idea, so they began to make plans. 'I will get some names of old people and next week we can send them an invitation,' said Miss Green. 'During the week you think about what we can give them for a present.' John ran to Mummy after to tell her all the plans and she promised to help.

Next week there was such a lot to talk about when they met at church. Miss Green had the name of an old lady who lived by herself, and also of a crippled lady and her husband who were very poor and never went out. John's mother had heard of a blind man who was lonely. That made four people they could help. They began to colour some invitation cards which Miss Green had bought for them and then they all wrote their names, and put the cards in the envelopes ready to post them.

'Now,' said Miss Green, 'what are we going to give them as a present, and what are we going to do with them when they come?' John had been talking to his mother about this and he said, 'My Mummy thinks they would like a Christmas parcel of things they could have to eat on Christmas Day.'

'That's a good idea, John,' said Miss Green. 'I suggest we all bring something for the parcels next week; it could be tea, tinned fruit, biscuits, or anything you think they would like.' 'Could we make a decoration to go on their tables?' John asked. 'Yes, John,' said Miss Green, 'we can do that next week too.' 'When they come, can we act the Christmas story and sing them carols?' said Mary. 'That's a good idea,' said John and Miss Green together. 'We must get that ready next week too. Now it is time to go home, but first we will go the the pillar box and post the invitations.'

What a busy day it was next Sunday! All the children came with things for the parcel. John had been to the shops with his mother and with his own money bought a box of little cheeses, and his mother had bought some biscuits and tea. The others had brought tinned fruit, sugar, sweets and lots of other things, and Miss Green had made three small Christmas cakes with a robin on the top of each one. Everything was put in three piles and they began to make the decoration for the table.

Some stuck a small candle in each of three cheese boxes; others painted fir cones and leaves and then stuck them round the candle. 'They look very pretty,' thought John. Then they began to pack three big boxes Miss Green had brought for them to use.

While they were covering the boxes with pretty paper, John suddenly said, 'How are the old people going to get to us? They can't walk.' 'I expect I can get some people from church to collect them,' Miss Green said. 'Now we will put the boxes in the cupboard until next week and begin to practise the carols and the story we are going to act.' So they all worked very hard.

John was so excited during the week. He thought Sunday would never come; but it did at last. John got to church very early and helped the others get the room ready. They put big chairs out for the visitors and got the parcels out of the cupboard, but hid them behind the piano.

'Here they come!' shouted John, as he looked out of the window and saw the cars go past. The old people were soon in the room and John and the others showed them to their chairs. The children sang the carols and then acted the Christmas story. John made a good Joseph, and Mary had brought her own doll to be baby Jesus. Some of the others were shepherds and some Wise Men.

The Wise Men brought in the three boxes and gave them to the old people. How surprised they were! John watched them look inside, and saw the smiles on their faces as they saw the good things for them to take home. Then it was time to finish and the cars came to take the old people home. 'Goodbye, and thank you,' said the old people. 'Goodbye and a Happy Christmas,' said John and the others.

During Christmas Day John wondered if the old people

were enjoying their gifts, and when he went to church on Sunday, sure enough there were three letters waiting for them from the old people, saying a big thank you.

23

Christmas Eve in Bethlehem, 1972

I AM Munib, an Arab boy aged nine; living in Palestine and my twin sisters and I had such a happy Christmas Eve that we should like to tell you about it.

We live in Jerusalem with our parents and two older brothers, inside the crowded Old City. We and eighteen other Christian families live in tiny houses on a high wall around a little church. We are poor but we help each other and are happy to be safe after losing two homes in wars. If you came to see us my father would say 'Welcome; you are our brother, our sister, this is your home.' All Arabs welcome visitors.

Everyone we know goes to Bethlehem on Christmas Eve. Until now we three have gone by day with our mother, and our other brothers by night with our father. This year we were to join in everything as a family. When we were told this, the twins danced excitedly, but I felt too grown-up!

In the morning five little girl cousins and our aunt arrived. We walked through the narrow streets, and outside the grand western walls, got on a bus number twenty-two (this looks to you like two sevens backwards – so now you know an Arab figure). It goes along the ridge of the Judaean hills. Far below is the Dead Sea, and looking like a volcano, Herod's tomb. He did not live long after having the babies killed when he heard from the Wise Men about a new King of the Jews being born. (Did you know that only lately the bones of sixty-eight children have been found in a cave unopened before?)

Below Bethlehem we left the bus and carrying the youngest cousins on our backs galloped down the steep hill to what we call the 'Shepherds' Fields'. In one of the many caves we ate our flat rounds of unleavened bread, goat cheese, olives, and many nuts which we chew most of the time. Afterwards our brothers, wearing shepherds head-dresses, pretended we were their sheep, and we all copied the many shepherds going past, each with his flock.

At four o'clock my father read the story of the angels appearing to the shepherds. The gleam in the wintry sky made us think of 'the light that shone around'. At 4.30 crowds of people came to sing carols led by a choir of blind girls and 'Mamma', their head teacher. They were just back from England where they gave seventeen concerts. At five o'clock we all went back up the steep hill feeling we were hurrying to see the Baby. One huge star twinkled over the Fields.

At seven we had supper. There were many little veal chops (once my father surprised our English friend by suddenly saying 'This is little-cow – it is good' – he did not mind when we laughed).

With the chops we ate green beans and aubergines, and each of us had a bowl of homus (like thick yoghourt with herbs) and many rounds of the flat bread to dip in it. Arabs do not like sweet pastries. You do, don't you? We drank thick, black, sweet Turkish coffee from tiny cups. Afterwards my father read the rest of the Christmas stories.

At eight we all went to the special buses from Saint George's Anglican Cathedral, for only Christians may enter Bethlehem late on Christmas Eve. This rule is the sad result of wars. We saw the lights of a Christian village where the people had been barred from coming, as a gunman had been found there. Many groups were on the road, often a husband and a wife with a donkey, and dressed just like Joseph and Mary when they went to pay their taxes long ago. All buses stopped below the town.

Then we started on our task to help the blind girls from Helen Keller Home off the buses and guide them. I had to look after one called Mariam. I knew I was not to help too much; just make sure she avoided small trees and ruts in the rough road.

We reached the group of churches in Bethlehem which have been built where Mary and Joseph at last found a place to spend the night – you can see them in the pictures – the oldest with a low door to prevent anyone riding in and animals from straying there.

In the courtyard some Bethlehem boys were playing and I steered Mariam past. Blind people always seem happy; only when soldiers holding guns roared past in jeeps did she shrink away.

The main square was ablaze with light; an American choir was singing carols on a platform with crowds around. There were many police, and soldiers pointing guns, and even young men and girls shouting and mocking. But my father said that was better than when Jesus was born, for there were no worshippers then, only crowds hating having to pay Roman taxes.

We guided the girls to the left, into the quiet Greek court-yard, for the 'Nine Lessons and Carols' service, like you have in England in many of your churches at Christmas. First we took them down some awkward stairs to the place where, it is believed, Jesus must have been born.

The inn (or khan) which once stood there was a rough resting place for travellers – there are many remains of them in my country. In those days there was laughing, shouting, dice-throwing and even fighting. I am glad Jesus was born where the donkeys or horses or camels sheltered. Animals are understanding and they would have felt wonder.

We guided the girls to the big brass star on the ground, putting their hands through the hole to touch the ancient rock which may be the very spot where Jesus was born.

Opposite is a tiny chapel with a cradle where after midnight the 'baby' would be put as in your 'cribs'. Women of the Church in blue capes and white veils sang quietly.

After a prayer we went up to our carols; the Archbishop said how everyone longed for peace and must pray for it.

Someone else took Mariam back. I stood still. The big

star now twinkled over the Church and I remembered the Wise Men.

Crowds were pouring up for the Midnight Service at St. Catherines' whose bells you hear on the radio. I could not see our buses. They had gone without me. It was dreadful. I was tired and five miles was a long walk.

Suddenly the crowd cleared and I saw a bus and my mother looking about anxiously. I ran to her. She said gently that I had delayed others going to St. George's Midnight Service. I nearly said, 'But Jesus got lost', then remembered that he stayed behind to do good and I had just been thoughtless. So I said, 'I am sorry.'

The twins were asleep but they woke as the bells rang out over the countryside. Christmas Day had begun. People everywhere were saying, 'A Happy Christmas.' We turned and looked at floodlit Bethlehem and my father said quietly, 'The Light of the World.'

24

Festival of Lights

RACHEL and Helen were getting really excited about Christmas this year, because Gopal was coming to stay with them. 'We must make him very welcome,' said Mummy, 'because he is leaving his own family behind in India and coming to study in Britain. He has never been here before and he will want to know all about Christmas, and I expect he will tell us lots of interesting things about India.'

'Surely everybody knows about Christmas,' said Rachel. 'Yes, everybody knows we remember the birthday of Jesus at Christmas,' added Helen. Mummy shook her head. 'Gopal won't keep Christmas at his home in India,' she said, 'because his family are not Christians; they are Hindus, and they have their own Festivals.'

At last the day came for Gopal to arrive. While Daddy went to meet him, Rachel and Helen decided to get out the Christmas decorations, to make the house look gay and welcoming. The Christmas tree was ready for the tinsel and fairy lights to be hung on its branches, and the children, with Mummy's help, very carefully arranged them all over the tree.

Mummy had just switched on the fairy lights when they heard the front door, and they all went into the hall to meet Daddy and their visitor. After they had all been introduced, Mummy went to make some tea, and the children and Daddy showed Gopal into the room where the tree was sparkling with lights and tinsel. Gopal explained, 'How beautiful! Now that really reminds me of home.' 'Oh,' said Rachel, 'do you have Christmas trees with lights in India?' 'No,' Gopal replied, 'but we have our own Festival of Lights.' And while they were drinking tea, Gopal told them something about the Festival of Lights in India.

He told them that the Festival was held once a year, as

Christmas is in England. 'It begins as soon as darkness falls,' he said. 'We prepare for the Festival before the darkness comes, and we have all our lights ready in good time. As soon as it begins to get dark, everybody, no matter how poor, makes sure that they have some lights outside their houses. They put lights every few inches along their window ledges, on their roofs and by their doors. It looks so beautiful to see a whole village twinkling with little lights in the darkness. Everybody is excited and happy when the Festival comes.'

'Do you have electric lights?' asked Helen. 'Oh no,' replied Gopal, 'only the rich people can afford electric lights. Most people just have little saucers made out of clay. They pour in some oil, and then they twist up some cotton wool to make a wick. When the cotton has soaked up some of the oil they light it, and the light lasts as long as the wick lasts. Then, when all the lights are shining, everybody dances and sings, and there is lots of noise and enjoyment.' 'What fun,' said the children.

'Do you like playing with dolls?' Gopal asked them. 'Oh yes,' they said, 'we love doing that.' 'Well,' he said, 'we have lots of doll-makers in India, and they make dolls specially for the Festival. They make them out of clay, and paint them with very bright colours, and sell them in the streets. Most children have some at Festival time.'

'But why do people keep the Festival of Lights in this way?' asked Daddy. Gopal told them that the Festival was to remember the victory of good over evil. 'Long, long ago,' he said, 'there was a prince named Rama who married a beautiful princess called Sita, and they were very happy together. But one day some wicked people came and captured Sita and took her away. Rama was very sad, but he was determined to get her back, and he set out to rescue her. He had many adventures and faced many dangers, but at last, with the help of the monkey people, he did rescue her, and brought her back to his kingdom. There they were happy once more, and were crowned King and Queen.'

'So,' Gopal went on, 'the Festival celebrates this victory of good over bad, and the new beginning of Rama and Sita's happiness. And so everyone tries to make a new beginning at Festival time. For instance, a business man will start a new account book, or a housewife will get rid of all her old cooking pots and buy new ones.' Mummy thought this was a particularly good idea, and they all laughed!

'What a lovely Festival that must be!' said Mummy, 'so full of happiness and colour and excitement.'

'But now,' said Gopal, 'you tell me about your Festival and why you put lights on a tree.'

'We do it for Jesus' birthday,' said Rachel. Between them they went on to tell him about how Jesus was born in a stable in Bethlehem long ago, and how the shepherds were told by angels about his birth and came to worship him. Then they told Gopal about the Wise Men. 'They were guided to the stable by a star,' said Helen. 'Yes,' said Rachel, 'they had come ever such a long way, but God made sure that they would find the Baby Jesus at last.' 'And they had wonderful presents for him,' said Helen, 'Gold and frank – and frank—' 'Frankincense and myrrh,' said Mummy, to help her with the difficult words. 'Yes, that's it,' said Helen, 'and you see, we can't give gifts to Jesus himself, so we give them to each other instead.'

The next day was Christmas Day. At breakfast time the girls put the family presents on the table, all wrapped up in coloured paper, and of course Gopal was included in the family so he had parcels too. Rachel had made him a lovely calendar with a photograph of an English country scene that she had cut out of a magazine. Helen had knitted him a scarf to keep him warm during the English winter. They were very excited when they opened the presents he had brought for them – a pair of Indian slippers each, and in the slippers some brightly coloured dolls which he had bought for them at the Festival of Lights before he left India.

'I am glad to share your Festival of Lights with you,' he said.

25

The Gift that You Cannot See

MANY years ago in an old town of crooked streets and steep red roofs a little lad named Peter lived with his mother. Peter laughed and chattered and romped as boys will; while all day long, and often half the night long too, his mother knitted. 'Click-click-clitter' went those shining steel needles, for by her knitting Peter's mother earned shelter for herself and her little son, and enough to keep hunger from the door.

It was the time when shops are more brightly lit and stalls more gaily decked, though bitter winds blow and frosts bite keen: the time before the festival of the Christ Child's birth. Peter's mother, standing by the window of their attic room to catch the last faint gleams of winter daylight, saw her rosy-faced little son running down the street with the neighbour's children. Then she heard the clatter of his feet on the wooden stair, and he came in. At first he did not see her in the gloom, but though she had not spoken, the little lad laughed confidently.

'I know you are here, Mother,' he said. 'I can't see you, but I know you are here.'

So she came out from the dormer window. Mother and child ate bread together, with a little honey for the child; they drank water, and laughed to call it silver wine.

Then, 'Mother,' said Peter, 'it is Christmas Day tomorrow.'

'The Christ Child send you joy, little son,' said his mother. 'Tomorrow is indeed Christmas Day.' In her heart she sighed to think of the toys in the shops and the oranges on the stalls, and never a penny in her purse that would buy them for her child.

'The other children hang their stockings tonight,' said Peter, big eyes bright with anticipation. 'Mother, may I hang up my stocking?'

To the child's eager questioning face she nodded.

'You shall indeed hang your stocking, little son,' she said. Peter clapped his hands. She stooped and kissed his tumbled flaxen hair. Then she said to him suddenly:

'Give it to me!'

'Give what?' asked Peter.

'The kiss I gave you,' said his mother.

Peter put a puzzled hand to his head. 'It isn't there . . . I haven't got it . . . yes, I have . . . no . . .'

'Did I not give it you, little son?'

'Oh, yes,' he nodded vigorously. 'Funny Mummy!' he said, and began tugging off the striped stocking of her knitting which he wore. 'You can't see kisses,' he said.

She lifted him to her knee, and helped the stocking off over the turn of his sturdy heel. Together they hung it from the chimney shelf above the dying embers. Then they sat down again, the child on her lap. Together they spoke of the joys of Christmas, of how they would wake to the ringing of all the bells in the town, of the carols they would sing with the neighbour's children, of the games they would play, of merriment and of jollity. Last of all they spoke of the stocking hanging in the candlelight above the embers.

'Remember, Peter,' she said, 'You could not see my kiss, when it was truly yours. Perhaps God will bring you his best gift of all, the gift that you cannot see.'

Then, for the child was drowsy, they said the night prayer together, and she laid him to sleep, wrapped in her brown petticoat against the chilly air.

Very early before the dawn, the bells of the old town began to ring for the festival of the Christ Child's birth; and very early Peter awoke. The embers were dead now, but above them from the chimney shelf a striped stocking hung. Up from the hard bed he sprang, and ran across the boards in his bare feet. By standing a-tip-toe he could reach it. He bent over the stocking. Then, all starry eyed, he flung himself upon his mother.

'Mother, Mother! wake up, wake up! The bells are ringing, and oh, Mother, he has brought it, the best gift of all! My stocking is full to the very brim of the gift that I cannot see!'

Now of all the Christmas gladness in the old town with the crooked streets and steep red roofs, none was more joyous than the gladness that day of Peter and his mother. When Peter ran down to sing carols with the neighbour's children, he took with him his precious gift.

'Why do you bring that empty stocking?' asked the neighbour's wife as she saw them off from her door. Peter let her peep. 'It isn't empty,' he whispered. 'It's full to the brim of the best gift of all, the gift that you cannot see.' The kindly neighbour shook a bewildered head.

The Mayor in his grand house by the market square sat alone at his Christmas breakfast. He heard the sound of children's voices a-carolling, and went to the window. When the children saw him they called shrilly, 'We wish you happy, sir!' One of them waved to him an empty stocking, tight gripped in a small frost-roughened hand. Now, though the Mayor was a grim man, he too had awakened to the sound of the bells; and he took brown pence from his pouch and went down to give alms to the children who sang. 'What is this empty stocking you hold?' he asked of the smallest child.

'Look!' said the child, as one who shares a wonderful secret. The grim Mayor stooped to look. The youngest child danced for very joy. 'It is full to the very brim with the best gift of all,' he said. 'The gift that you cannot see.'

The Mayor straightened himself. He noted the child's thin shoes and threadbare clothes. 'And is this a happy Christmas for you?' he asked, and his voice was scarcely grim at all.

The child nodded, capering in the snow. 'Oh yes, yes, yes!' he said. Then he asked, with a child's ready friendliness, 'Did you have the best gift of all, too – the gift that you cannot see?'

The Mayor hesitated. 'Perhaps I had it, but I knew not,' he said at last.

Now during that day the Mayor inquired and learnt

where the child lived who had come a-carolling. Because of one small child's shining eyes, he could not rest by his own fireside that Christmas evening. He remembered the thin shoes, and the threadbare clothes, even while he remembered the joyful young voice and the stocking that was so precious.

Therefore, at last, just after dusk, he went out. Coming without noise up a certain stair, he found an attic door ajar. One candle was alight within, to show a poor bare room, very clean, with a few dying embers on the hearth and a crust of bread on the table. But the light of the candle showed a mother as she crooned the Lullaby of the Stable to a sleepy little lad, who still held a striped stocking.

As he watched and listened, the lullaby ceased, for the child had fallen asleep. The mother laid the child on the bed, and the Mayor saw that he was wrapped against the cold in the woman's own brown petticoat. Moving to take up her knitting, she became aware of him, and smoothed her apron quickly and would have curtseyed. He restrained her.

He brought in a basket and spoke softly for fear of rousing the child. In a moment he was gone, and she stood gazing after him, left with the basket and five gold pieces, and the memory of his words: 'Far more than this have you, in that little son of yours, who can receive the best gift of all. Yet for the sake of his sharing with me of the greater gift, accept, I ask you, this the lesser gift.'

26

Ithar's Gift

In a little village the people were all making ready for Christmas Day. For a long time before this they had been thinking about it, for it was the custom in those parts that every year each should bring to the church on Christmas Day some gift for the Christ-child.

Some brought gifts of food and clothing that were given away afterwards to the very poorest people of the village, for had he not said, 'Inasmuch as ye have done it unto the least of these my brethren ye have done it unto me'? Others brought gifts to make his church beautiful.

So in the spring the shepherd would set apart a lamb, whose wool should be shorn later to be a gift. The farmer would store some grain or apples. The shoemaker would make a pair of little shoes. The smith would beat out a candlestick for the church. The carpenter would make a wooden footstool. The weaver would weave the material for a curtain. The wise scholar who lived in the big house on the hill would write a hymn of praise, and the fiddler would set it to music. The artist who lived in the little cottage in the valley would paint a picture of our Lord as he lay in the stable on the first Christmas night with the shepherds looking on, or as he sat on his mother's knee when the Wise Men came bringing their gifts. The old women knitted warm scarves and shawls. The younger embroidered the weaver's curtain. The children brought gifts, too, nuts and berries they had gathered in October and stored – holly and evergreens, gathered from many a thorny hedge and difficult place; and those who were a little older brought a few of the bright pennies they had saved from their earnings.

Now there was a man in the village who had made ready no gift. His name was Ithar, and he was a gipsy.

He was a queer, wild man, who did odd jobs for the

farmers, or indeed anywhere where anyone would give him food and shelter for the work he did. He was so poor that he never had a penny to spend; his clothes were old and tattered; his shoes nearly worn out. The children of the village were frightened of him, and ran away when they saw him; the dogs barked at him; no one loved him very much, for he was a surly man, who spoke little, and crossly when he did.

But as Christmas drew near, and Ithar saw the people making ready their gifts, he began to be ashamed that he had nothing to give.

It was Christmas Eve, and a clear frosty night, when Ithar was coming back from the farm where he had been working, and passed the little church. All was dark inside the church, except for one little lamp that burnt like a rosy star. When Ithar saw it he went and knelt down there in the quiet darkness and prayed.

When he looked up he saw the people had made a little stable in one part of the church and there they had put little images of the mother and father and the holy Babe. On one side there were the shepherds offering their lambs, and on the other the Wise Men offering their crowns.

Then Ithar said, 'Lord, I am sorry I have nothing to give.'

It was just as if a quiet voice out of the darkness answered: 'Ithar, give me your heart.'

When Ithar heard that, he answered: 'How shall I give my heart, Lord?'

The voice said: 'When your heart is kind you will know that you have given it to me.'

Then Ithar rose up quickly and went out into the night. He had not gone far before he heard a sound of crying, and he saw a little child who had lost his way. 'Tell me where you live and I will take you,' said Ithar.

At first the little child was frightened at Ithar's gipsy face, but heard that his voice was kind, so he let himself be lifted on his shoulder and carried home. 'A blessing on your kind heart this holy night,' said the mother, when she saw Ithar and her little lost son. She would have called him in to rest, but he went on his way quickly.

As he reached the hill that led to his home he saw an old woman carrying a big bundle of wood to make a Christmas fire. 'Let me carry that for you,' said Ithar. At first the old woman was a little frightened, but when she looked in his eyes she saw they were kind, so she handed the bundle to him, and he carried it for her up the hill. At the top she thanked him, saying: 'A blessing on your kind heart this holy night.'

Next day the church was filled with people all singing their Christmas praises. The shepherds were there, the farmers, the shoemaker, the carpenter, the weaver, the smith, the scholar, the artist, old men and women, and young boys and girls and little children – all had brought their gifts and all were happy. There was a little boy there who smiled at Ithar, and an old woman who nodded kindly to him in the porch.

During the service they sang a favourite carol which they had every year. This is its last verse:

> What can I give him, poor as I am?
> If I were a shepherd, I would bring a lamb,
> If I were a wise man, I would do my part;
> Yet what I can I give him – give my heart.

And Ithar, not standing with the rest but kneeling there in his pew, was happier than any of them, for he too had brought his gift. He knew that he had given his heart.

27

A New Carol

MARIA and Johann had been to choir practice. It was Christmas Eve, and the sun was already setting as they left the Church of St. Nicholas and walked through the snow to their home in the Austrian village of Oberndorf, near Salzburg.

Mother had tea ready for them. 'You must be cold and ready for something hot to drink,' she said. 'Did you have a good choir practice?'

Maria looked at Johann, but fortunately, before either had time to reply, Mother went on, 'It's a shame about the organ. Herr Gruber plays so beautifully. Fancy a mouse nibbling holes in the bellows just before Christmas! Young Pastor Mohr will be so disappointed that we can't have the organ for our midnight service. The singing won't be the same without it.'

Johann kicked Maria under the table. Surprisingly, neither of them seemed very upset about the organ. They'd had an extremely good choir practice. But that was a secret they were determined to keep – at any rate until after midnight.

The blanket of snow made everything very quiet and still that night, and the children listened with mounting excitement for the sound of the church bells.

'I can hear them,' Johann called out at last, and the children put on their warmest clothes and set out with Mother and Father towards the church. When they went through its doorway, Maria held her breath. The church looked so beautiful, glowing in the soft, warm light of candles.

There was silence in the church while Pastor Mohr announced that the organ was out of order. Then the silence was broken as everyone craned forward to see why Herr

Gruber had walked out to the front. Surely he was not going to try to play the organ after all! No, not the organ. That was a guitar in his hands.

Now the pastor and the organist began to sing, and for the first time the villagers heard the words of a new carol that had been written specially for them.

> 'Still the night, holy the night!
> Sleeps the world; hid from sight,
> Mary and Joseph in stable bare
> Watch o'er the Child beloved and fair,
> Sleep in heavenly rest.'

Franz Gruber played the accompaniment on his guitar, and the choir sang the new carol, their voices singing to a whisper in the last line, 'Sleeping in heavenly rest.'

On their way home after the service, Maria and Johann told their mother and father all about the new carol.

'It was the other night,' said Johann, 'that Pastor Mohr was walking home through the snow, thinking how quiet and still our village looked. Perhaps, he thought, it had been like this in the hills round Bethlehem on the night Jesus was born.'

'And he made a poem about it,' burst in Maria. 'As soon as he got home he wrote it down on a piece of paper. He was so excited about it that he went out again in the snow, even although it was very late – early yesterday morning, in fact – and walked all the way to Herr Gruber's house in Arnsdorf.'

'Yes,' went on Johann, 'and Herr Gruber liked it so much that he composed a tune for it, and he played the tune on his guitar. Then yesterday afternoon at choir practice, they sang it to us, and we learnt it so that we could sing it at the midnight service.'

'And that's the end of the story,' said Maria.

But it wasn't the end of the story! Some time later, a man came from another village to repair the organ. When he had finished his work, he asked Herr Gruber to test the organ by playing a tune on it. What do you think he played? Yes, the new carol, 'Still the night'.

The repair man was so delighted with it that he asked for a copy of the words and music. In no time at all, the carol became very popular in his own village of Zillertal. Four sisters who lived there gave concerts in towns all over Austria, and wherever they went they sang, 'Still the night'. Soon everybody was singing this beautiful carol.

It is more than 150 years since it was written on that Christmas Eve, and during those years it has become a favourite with people all over the world.

28

The White Gifts

THERE once lived an old man who possessed a wonderful fiddle, but its wonders were only seen at Christmas-tide. Every Christmas Eve he would steal out of the city gates with his fiddle under his arm and make his way to a tree standing bare and leafless under the winter sky. He would wait until there was no one in sight, then he would draw his bow across the strings – and at once the most wonderful music floated out into the cold, wintry air. As he played on, the sleeping life in the tree above him began to stir. White buds came on the bare black branches and presently these opened into beautiful white blossoms. Then the white petals began to fall until the frozen ground beneath the tree was covered with them, looking like a white mantle of pure, driven snow. Still the old man played on, until, where there had been flowers, there now hung wonderful sweet-smelling white fruit.

Now the old fiddler changed his tune. His music had a call – a lilt with it. Out of the city gate came the children, leaping, laughing and dancing. They swept along, dancing, as they came, until they surrounded the tree, and linking their hands in a great ring, danced around while the old man played. Suddenly, on a shrill note, the music stopped and, as though it were a signal, down dropped the white fruit upon the ground.

At once the ring of children broke up and they ran eagerly forward, each to pick up a white gift. And the old fiddler smiled as he watched the children returning to the city, each one carrying a white gift for Christmas Day. And the special wonder of the gift was that each held what the child really wanted.

Now it so happened that the fiddler's magic music provided always one more gift than there were children to receive them. And the boys and girls loved to settle among

95

themselves what should be done with the extra gift. Sometimes they sent it to a crippled child or to one who was ill
and so could not join the white gift dance.

So when one Christmas Eve the children discovered
that there was none left over, the boys and girls looked at the
old man in wide-eyed surprise. What could have happened?
But the old fiddler looked stern, his smiles had disappeared.
Putting his fiddle underneath his chin he played again. A
strange, grieved tone was in the music and one boy began
to look very uncomfortable. He slipped off home by himself
as though anxious not to be seen. And when that boy got
home and opened his white gift, he got a shock. Instead of
finding within it the usual good things, it was empty. He
took from under his coat a second gift – the extra one he had
greedily stolen – and that was empty too!

As the other children were going home, surprised that
there had been no extra gift that Christmas Eve, they noticed
that one girl was crying bitterly. On the evening before,
Rose – for that was her name – had seen a poor, homeless
man and woman, tired and hungry, come into the city.
Unable to pay for poorest lodgings or humblest food, they
had taken refuge in a tumble-down shed not far from where
she lived, and that morning a little baby boy had been born
to the homeless pair. So Rose cried because she had wanted
to see the extra white gift given to the little child of the
friendless strangers.

'If only there had been another gift,' she sighed when she
reached home and stood looking at her treasure. Then a
sudden thought came to her. 'As there is no extra gift for the
little mite, should I not give my own gift to him?'

Rose tried hard to put the thought out of her mind, but
back it came again and again. At last, 'Yes, I will give it,' she
said, and was surprised to find that with the resolve there
came great happiness. She *wanted* to give her own gift!

Running as fast as she could, so that the baby should have
the white gift as soon as possible, she reached the tumble-
down shelter, and tapped timidly on the door.

'Come in!' called a sweet voice.

Rose pushed the door open and peeped in. Huddled up in a corner for warmth the poor woman was sitting, nursing her baby, while the man stood near, watching them both. The woman's face was so sweet and kind that Rose lost all fear. She stepped into the hut and held out the white gift. 'It's for the baby,' she said.

The mother took it with a look of pleased surprise. She unfolded the baby's tiny hand from the shawl, and Rose placed the gift within his wee fingers.

She stayed a short while, talking to the mother and father and watching the baby. Then, with a shy smile, she got up and left the hut.

In the church that Christmas the manger scene had been set up as it always was. But this year there was a difference. Among those offering gifts were not only shepherds and wise men, but other townspeople, including some boys and girls.

One of Rose's friends pointed to the children.

'I wish I had been there, bringing a gift like they are.'

Rose said nothing, but as she thought of the tumble-down shed and her white gift in the baby's hands, she found herself thinking, 'I feel it is just as if I gave it to Jesus himself.'

D

29

The Picture that brought Peace

It was late for travellers to be on the road; the sun had set and already the clear outline of the city-fortress on the hill was lost in the deep shadow. The tall trees against the skyline looked dark and menacing and challenging to wayfarers approaching the guarded gates of the city. Yet the solitary horseman on the steep hill track urged his mount steadily forward, seemingly unperturbed by the lateness of the hour or the grimness of the prospect. But no one knew better than he the perils of the way.

For the rival cities of England were at war with each other· The ducal families who were the virtual heads of the rival cities had invested their servants and followers with arms, and turned their palaces into fortresses. Nobles from other towns forsook their homes and joined forces with one or other of the two factions. The whole countryside was under arms, and constant forays and skirmishes took place on the highways.

But this traveller had no fears for his safety. He even whistled a gay little street song as he put his horse to the last steep slope before the gates. Scarcely had he done so when the sentry's challenge rang out, 'Who goes there?'

With a clash of arms a hoarse voice bade him rein in his horse. The gates opened a crack and a man-at-arms, holding a torch high, surveyed the traveller. 'Your name, and from whence come you?' Half smilingly the traveller replied, 'I am no enemy. I am the painter of churches.'

'The painter! Welcome! Enter; the Duke has asked for you.' The gateway widened, willing hands guided the traveller into the city. Every city coveted his presence; he might go where he would so long as he was willing to cover the white walls of their churches with his beautiful frescoes.

So for long months the painter stayed in the hill city, the one unarmed man in the throngs, untroubled by jealous loyalties or thoughts of revenge. Through the narrow, winding streets he went, making friends with the people, joking with the bloodthirsty soldiery, bargaining with shopkeepers, playing with the children. And all the while he was storing in his memory the gestures and looks of those with whom he talked and played. He loved to paint the things and people he saw, and so his friendliness and goodwill to all glowed again in lovely colour and form upon the church walls.

Seated high up on the walls, he would sometimes stop his work to watch the people kneeling at prayer far below. When the church rang with wonderful music and the air was heavy with the cloud of incense, he would see the symbol of Christ's Passion while every worshipper knelt in reverence. The haughty, proud and powerful nobles knelt, but in full armour and grasping their swords, while the pike and spears carried by their bodyguards flashed in the soft candle-light of the high altar.

To the painter's way of thinking such worship was unreal. The stern, proud faces of these fighting men did not inspire his brush. As he turned to his work again, thoughts of the sweet-faced women he had seen busy about their everyday tasks, preparing food, tending to their children, filled his mind. He smiled at the recollection of the children at their play, and he knew what picture he would paint to beautify the church wall. No grand design in which would figure the great nobles who warred on each other should glow upon the wall, but the story of the first 'Christ Mass', with the tiny baby Jesus held in the arms of a peasant woman, while kings and wise men knelt in true adoration.

So day after day the painter worked away while the useless war raged on, victory first to one faction then to the other. Meanwhile Christmas-tide drew near. The Duke, the painter's patron, was eager for the frescoe to be finished and shown during the festive season. He was planning a campaign against the enemy city to take place as soon as the worst of the winter was past, and wished the matter of the frescoe to be hurried on. Not even he knew what had been pictured, nor was the Duke very particular. To be able to point to the work as that of the famous artist was sufficient for him, although he expected that the painter would portray him in some noble attitude. The citizens rather enjoyed the air of mystery surrounding the subject of the picture, for the painter's workmen were faithful and kept their master's secret.

Christmas Eve came, and with pomp and ceremony the cloth veiling the frescoed wall was taken down. Proud heads craned, men stood on tiptoe, mothers held the children high so that they might see. There was a loud murmur of admiration as the veiling cloth fell and the lovely colours were revealed. Then came a long silence, broken by a childish voice, 'See! There's the little Lord Jesus, and his face is like the face of our baby!'

All tongues were released as the crowd swayed to obtain a nearer view. 'The child speaks truly. The blessed Babe is a child of our own people. And the Blessed Virgin – she, too, is one of us.'

As for the Duke, he gazed strangely upon the familiar story pictured in such homely guise. Even to his proud, self-sufficient soul the beauty and naturalness made its appeal. He read in the adoring, self-forgetful homage of the pictured kings such worship as he had never offered. He turned to his bodyguard, gave a brief order, and every man laid down his pike upon the floor. The church walls echoed to the clash and clang, followed by a great silence, whilst the wondering onlookers strained to see what would happen next.

Then the Duke, removing his feathered cap and unbuckling his sword, knelt at the feet of the pictured Babe, and in a moment came a long, subdued rustling as everyone in the building joined the Duke in an act of homage that was a real celebration of the first Christmas.

A few days later the snow had melted on the hills, the way

was open for travelling and the painter went on his way, back to his city, and as he went he sang for very gladness:

'O Come, all ye faithful, joyful and triumphant.'

The spring campaign had been abandoned. His Christmas picture had proclaimed goodwill to all.

30

On Christmas Day in the Morning

(*A Missionary Story*)

JOHN BAXTER was a shipwright, and he lived in Chatham. He was one of the many who had been thrilled and changed by John Wesley's message. One day John Baxter was sent for.

'They are wanting a Government shipwright in Antigua, Mr. Baxter; I am instructed to offer the post to you.'

Honest John Baxter had never thought of leaving England; he asked for a little time to consider the matter. Antigua; why, that was where Mr. Wesley's friend, Mr. Gilbert, had lived. Had not Mr. Wesley said that since Mr. Gilbert's death the Christian slaves there had been left without a helper?

'If I take this job, and go out to Antigua,' thought John Baxter, 'I might be able to help them a little.'

Baxter sought out John Wesley, and talked the matter over; Wesley urged him to accept the post. So John Baxter sold up his home and said goodbye to his friends, and sailed for Antigua – not a missionary, you notice, but just a carpenter to help other people to follow Jesus Christ.

What a welcome the Christian slaves in Antigua gave the newly arrived carpenter when they found that he was ready to do what he could for them! John Baxter soon was spending every Sunday, and every evening after his work in the ship-yards was over, telling the stories of Jesus. He would ride out into the country; and, their day's work on the plantations over, the slaves would tramp six, seven, eight miles to meet their friend. Drenched with the tropical dew, they would stand together and forget their weariness as they spoke, or heard, or sang about the Lord Jesus.

So the months and years passed, until 1786 was nearly

ended. On Christmas Day in the morning, very early, a ship dropped anchor in the calm, warm water of Antigua Bay.

Her story was a strange one. She had been bound originally for Nova Scotia, away to the north, but fierce storms had interrupted the voyage and driven her far from her course. The captain had decided to change his plans and run for Antigua. His passengers, after the perils and discomforts of the stormy voyage, were more than thankful to be in calm harbourage at last.

'Christmas morning!' said one of them, coming up on to the deck early and looking across the still water at the white houses among the palm trees. 'Captain, could you give us a boat and put us ashore? I and my friends would be most grateful for the chance to keep this Christmas fitly on shore, with others who honour it as the birthday of our Master.'

The captain was ready to be obliging, for he had come to respect greatly the little man who spoke. Very soon the ship's boat was taking four passengers ashore. They landed on the quiet quay in the early morning sunlight, three young Methodist preachers, with their leader, Dr. Coke, a friend of John Wesley's.

'This is very different from the cold mists of Nova Scotia, where we had expected to do the Lord's work,' we can imagine Dr. Coke saying. 'But we thank God indeed for bringing us safely here. I wonder where the church or chapel may be? We must inquire.'

At that very moment John Baxter, the carpenter, was leaving his house on his way to the early morning service he had planned as Christmas celebration for his slave friends. As he left his house he noticed the unfamiliar ship riding at anchor, and idly wondered what it was. He turned a bend in the road and found himself face to face with – Dr. Coke! Baxter knew him as a friend of John Wesley's and a well-known leader.

You can just imagine how astonished, and how tremendously glad, the carpenter-missionary was. Never had a happier surprise marked a Christmas morning. Three times that Christmas Day Dr. Coke told the Christmas story to gatherings of slaves and their masters, there in Antigua. For the wealthy folk of the island were amazed by the Christmas visitor.

'He is an Oxford Doctor of Law, I hear,' one planter said to another.

'Yes, and a most eloquent and charming gentlemen,' his friend had to agree.

'One may ignore the stupid habits of a ship's carpenter,' said a third in lofty tones, 'but this gentleman seems to be a very distinguished clergyman indeed. I shall certainly go to hear him, and feel it my duty to do so.'

Before he left the island Dr. Coke had received a formal invitation to remain permanently as its parish minister. He could not do that, for he was pledged to do other Christian work. But he could, and did, go with John Baxter round the island, and to other small islands, exploring the great possibilities for the work there. So great were these opportunities that he left his three young helpers behind and sailed on himself. But he did not forget the needs of Antigua.

When he got back to England Dr. Coke told of those needs to all the societies of people at home who had found new joy and courage through John Wesley's preaching. He told them of John Baxter and his work. He reminded them of the wonderful story that lay behind the Christmas meeting, beginning with Mr. Gilbert's work there, and going on till it ended so strangely through a storm which drove a ship out of its way. He reminded them of the hundreds of people away in Antigua, and in other places, who were waiting to hear the Christmas story and feel the Christmas joy. From what he told them sprang the first overseas missionary work of the Methodist Churches.

31

The Surprise Brother

(*A West African Story*)

'WHAT happened?' asked Ojo, bewildered and drowsy. He fumbled with the damp, white plaster on his leg.

'The lorry crashed. Don't you remember?'

Remi wore a bandage round her black, curly hair and one of her eyes was almost closed up. Ojo thought crossly how silly she looked, all lop-sided. He glowered at her, the crossness getting mixed up with his headache and the discomfort of the plaster.

'I know your big basket of yams fell on my head. Why did you bring so many?'

Remi wondered why he must be so horrid, when they were the only two people in the ward from their home village. After all, they were class-mates even though not close friends.

'We were going to spend Christmas with my grandmother,' she explained, 'and Mother always takes her what she can from the farm. Were you going somewhere for the Festival?'

'For New Year,' said Ojo scornfully, 'not for your little festival.'

He felt sore and shaky, and miserable that the first real journey in all his ten years should end like this. He wanted to hit back at someone, and Remi was nearest.

'It isn't a *little* festival for us Christians,' Remi answered quickly. 'It's the day the Saviour was born.'

Ojo wasn't interested. His family followed the old religion.

'Where are we?' he demanded. 'And where is Mrs. Ajayi? She was to take me to my uncle's house in the city.'

'Another lorry came by and took the people like Mrs. Ajayi who weren't hurt. And we came here in an ambulance.'

Remi named a town unknown to Ojo, for they were nearly
100 miles from home.

When a nurse came to give them some medicine and to
settle them for the night, Remi asked how her mother was,
and was told she was all right.

'You may see her in the morning,' said the nurse, and
Remi smiled gratefully. She lent across to whisper to Ojo:
'My Mother is going to—' but Ojo rolled over as far as his
plaster would allow and pulled the blanket over his head.
He didn't want to know about Remi's mother. He had
enough miseries of his own.

By morning, Ojo felt much better. As he ate his breakfast
of corn porridge and fried bean cakes, he imagined himself
soon on his way to the city. But when the doctor came round,
she said that he must stay for at least a week.

'Till New Year's Eve?' cried Ojo. The doctor smiled
encouragingly.

'I hope you will enjoy spending Christmas with us,' she
said. She called it 'The Feast of the birth of Jesus'.

'I'm not a believer,' said Ojo sullenly. 'I don't know about
your Jesus.'

'Then we must tell you about him, for he's your Jesus
too,' said the doctor, and passing on called cheerfully, 'Good
morning, Remi. There's good news for you.'

'Why should Remi have good news?' sulked Ojo, and he
put his fingers in his ears. He felt alone and forgotten, so far
from his family. He spent the day lying glum and silent,
turning his head away whenever Remi tried to speak to
him and refusing to join the other children who were
helping the nurses to decorate the ward with paper garlands,
big stars and plaited palm leaves.

But by evening he had had enough of his own company,
and when a nurse wheeled up a chair with a plank to support
his leg, he allowed himself to be helped into it and wrapped
in a blanket.

A crowd had gathered in the centre of the compound,
where a low building with a long verandah gleamed white

in the moonlight and the feathery shapes of palm trees showed black against the sky. As the crowd, muffled in cloths against the cool night air, made room for Ojo's chair in the front row, drums began to beat, beaded gourds rattled, and the singing began.

> He is coming, our Brother!
> He is coming, God's Son!
> He is coming; get ready!

The crowd sang and swayed to the rhythm and against his will Ojo felt a thrill of excitement. There was going to be something to watch. He had never seen television, never been to the cinema; he was ready to be carried into the heart of the play, and as it went on, he forgot it was a play. He was there, in the middle of it, gripped by a story he had never heard properly before.

He saw the young girl, with the waterpot on her head, stopped by the tall young man in a flowing robe who gave her the amazing news that she was to be the mother of God's Son. He suffered with the weary travellers turned away from the hotel and sighed with relief when the hotel-keeper's wife reappeared and beckoned the young woman and her husband behind the curtain at the end of the verandah, driving out a perky brown goat and two idignant hens. He shivered with joyful terror with the cattle-men encamped outside the town, to whom the shining young man brought the wonderful news that was for everybody.

Again the voices sang, this time a soft tune of hope and mystery. The music ended, and suddenly from behind the curtain came the high, quavering wail of a newborn child. A great sigh broke from the crowd and, as the cattle-men hurried up, the curtain was drawn aside and there sat the young mother, her face alight with joy, and in her arms a small bundle with a dark head and one small, pinky-brown hand waving from the blue wrapper. A newborn hand.* The

* African babies are usually pale when they are born. Later, their skin becomes darker.

cattle-men knelt and some people in the crowd knelt too as the choir raised their voices in the final, exultant song:

> He is here, our Brother,
> Rejoice, and adore him!

Back in the ward was Remi, her face aglow. She saw the change in Ojo.

'Wasn't it wonderful?' she cried. 'To think that my brother should be the Lord Jesus!'

'*Your* brother?' asked Ojo sharply.

'Yes, I've been trying to tell you all day. My Mother's baby was born early this morning, and the nurses asked if she would mind lending him because the baby in the play must look newborn.' She looked at Ojo's suddenly clouded face. 'It's all right,' she said gently. 'Jesus was a real baby. He's your Brother, too. He's everybody's Brother.'

Suddenly Ojo smiled.

'Then that makes you my sister,' he said.

32

The Other Wise Man

EVERYONE has heard of the Three Wise Men who saw a star in the East and finally reached the manger in Bethlehem. But some say there was a fourth, and nothing in the Bible says there could not have been, because no number is mentioned.

His name, they say, was Artaban. Like the other three, he was an astrologer who believed he could read messages in the stars. Like them, he was sure that this new star they had all seen was so unusual that it must mean the birth of someone who would be very important indeed.

So when Melchior, Caspar and Balthasar planned a rendezvous where they would set out on their journey, Artaban agreed to meet them. He prepared a gift to take with him. Jewels, the most beautiful and valuable he could find. He was a rich man and he had often wondered how best he could use his wealth. Now, at last, he was sure the chance had come.

Very carefully he worked out how many days it would take to reach the rendezvous. Then he set out, riding fast on his journey. He had left nothing to chance. He would get there on time.

But Artaban had not allowed for the old man he saw lying ill by the roadside. A flicker of hope could be seen in the sick man's eyes as the stranger galloped past. Artaban had seen that look and in the brief moment of passing had read the man's thoughts. 'Someone who will take care of me? Ah no, he won't stop, not a rich man like him?'

'I must not stop,' thought Artaban. 'I shall be late and the others will not wait; why should they? I *cannot* stop.'

But he reined his horse to a halt and then turned it round. He dismounted and knelt beside the old man. He was friend-less and far from home, and very ill. Artaban summoned help, saw that the old man was properly looked after and paid for all that was needed. It took time, and one of his precious jewels had to be sold. But if his money helped to cure the sufferings of the sick, surely it was well spent?

Anxious now to make up time, Artaban rode hard. He came to another village and saw a great commotion outside one of its small cottages. Sitting on a bundle of blankets and clothing was a woman crying bitterly, clasping two small children in her arms. Her husband was arguing fiercely with a man who seemed to be driving him away from the cottage. A small crowd of neighbours were joining in the argument and adding to the general confusion.

Again Artaban forced himself to look ahead and ride on. But again he pulled up his horse, returned to the cottage and demanded to know what was happening.

'He has turned me out of my home,' exclaimed the husband. 'We have nowhere to go.'

'If he would pay his rent, he could stay,' retorted the man.

'I have promised to pay a little,' the husband persisted, 'and the whole of my debt as soon as I get work. I am willing to work, but if there is none . . .' And he spread his hands in despair.

When Artaban left the village some time later, another jewel had been sold. But if the money stayed a mother's tears and gave an honest man time to find work again, surely it was well spent?

Meanwhile, the other three Wise Men, having waited and waited at the rendezvous, could delay no longer. When Artaban reached the place and found them gone, he set out on the journey alone.

He did reach Bethlehem, as the others had done, only to learn that they had already left on their return journey. But Bethlehem and all the surrounding country was in an uproar. Artaban soon learned the reason – the cruel decree from Herod himself that all baby boys of two years old and under should be sought out and killed. Herod was determined that, if a 'king of the Jews' had indeed been born – as the Wise Men had declared, the child should not survive.

Artaban was deeply shocked. What could he do to save at least some of these helpless infants? The soldiers! They had their orders and were heartless enough to carry them out. But no doubt they were greedy too. Money would make them stay their hand. It did. More of Artaban's precious jewels had to be sold, but if the money saved the lives of little children, surely it was well spent?

News of his kindness spread like wildfire. Hungry people, homeless people, people wrongly imprisoned, people with clothes too ragged to keep out the cold or protect them from the fierce heat of the sun – all turned to Artaban and none was turned away.

But even Artaban's money, wealthy man though he was, could not last for ever, and the time came when he had no more to give away. The jewels which were to have been his gift to the infant King were all gone.

Artaban often thought about that gift. 'He never received it,' he thought, a little sadly.

But one day, when he was now an old man, Artaban heard about Jesus. Crowds gathered wherever he spoke. Many people said quietly to one another that here at last was the Messiah, the King who was to come.

Artaban's inquiries soon convinced him that this was the baby of Bethlehem, now grown to manhood. He went one day to listen to him. He was fascinated by what he heard. But certain words seemed to be spoken directly to him.

'When I was hungry, you gave me food, when thirsty, you gave me drink; when I was a stranger you took me into your home, when naked you clothed me; when I was ill, you came to my help, when in prison you visited me: anything you did for one of my brothers here, however humble, you did for me.'

Artaban thought about the gift for the baby of Bethlehem. 'I thought he had never received it. But now I know that he did.'

33

The Real Santa Claus

'I DON'T believe in any of that Santa Claus stuff.' Nigel's voice was scornful. But Hans, his friend from Holland, seemed to prick up his ears.

'Santa Claus, Santa Claus,' he repeated slowly. Then, turning to Nigel's parents, he said, 'Is that what you call our Saint Nicholas?'

'Yes, Hans, you're quite right. We have a way of altering words and names like that, I'm afraid,' replied Nigel's father.

Hans turned back to his friend. 'Don't you remember, last year when you came to stay with us? The bishop, and Black Peter, and the procession and . . . everything?'

Nigel and Hans were very good friends. It had all begun when a party of Dutch children had come to England for a holiday and Nigel's parents were among those who offered to look after one of the visitors. Not long after, Nigel had been invited to stay in the small town in Holland where Hans and his family lived. They had been to one another's homes several times.

Now Nigel looked at his friend's excited face and remembered every moment of the day Hans had spoken about.

It was early December and he was on a visit to Hans' home and one morning he had known as soon as they got up that there was something in the air. Something exciting was going to happen. He and Hans had not been allowed to leave the house. Everybody seemed to be waiting. But for what?

Suddenly, he heard the cry go up, 'Here he is! Here's Saint Nicholas!' All the house doors were opening and the children were pouring out on to the street. Along the street came a horse-drawn carriage. On one of the horses was perched a youth, his face, arms and hands blackened. He carried a birch, which he flourished threateningly at the boys and girls. But no one seemed to mind.

In the carriage sat an old man, dressed in a bishop's robes with a mitre on his head. His face was one of the kindest Nigel had ever seen.

Behind the carriage was a long procession of running, excited boys and girls. Hans grabbed Nigel and they joined the procession.

'Who is that, sitting in the carriage?' Nigel shouted to him above the noise. 'Saint Nicholas,' Hans answered. 'This is his day. He comes every year, and gives presents to us children – if we've been good,' he added with a grin. 'If we haven't, young Black Peter there sets about us with his birch, or is supposed to. But he never does.'

By now the carriage had stopped outside a house where a boy lived who couldn't come out with the rest because he was badly injured. He was brought to the door.

'Has he been good?' inquired the bishop, in a voice as kind as his face.

'Oh, yes,' smiled the boy's parents.

'Are you sure?' growled Black Peter, swishing his birch. The bishop did not wait for an answer, but brought out a present and gave it to the boy.

And so it went on, with the procession getting larger and larger, and stopping occasionally at a house where the child who lived there could not come out.

Then, in the market place, everyone gathered round.

'I have presents here for all good boys and girls,' called out the bishop.

'And I have this for all the naughty ones,' shouted Black Peter, waving his birch.

All the children of the town seemed to have been remarkably good because everyone got something, including Nigel.

When they got home again he had asked about this strange, kindly bishop. Centuries before such a bishop had really lived, Nigel was told, in Asia Minor. He found out where need was and then under cover of darkness took gifts of various kinds to needy homes. One day someone discovered where the mystery gifts came from.

Long after the good bishop died he was canonized, that is, made a Saint. People believed he still came and helped the needy, and the exciting morning in that small Dutch town, years later, owed its beginning to good Saint Nicholas.

Now, in his own home in England, a few days before Christmas, Nigel answered Hans' question. 'Yes, of course I remember. The Bishop – and Black Peter – presents for the children . . . It happens every year, doesn't it, at Christmas time?'

'Well not at Christmas,' said Hans. 'St. Nicholas Day is December 6th. But I suppose it's all the same really. He brings gifts – like the Santa Claus you don't believe in,' he added with a laugh.

'No, Hans, I don't think it *is* the same.' It was Nigel's father whose voice broke into the boys' conversation.

'Don't you?' said Nigel. 'Why not?'

'Tell me, Hans,' his father said. 'Your Saint Nicholas is meant to give presents to good boys and girls. Right?' Hans nodded.

'But everyone got a gift all the same,' put in Nigel.

'Because they bend the rules a bit. Isn't that so, Hans?'

'Afraid so,' said Hans with a grin.

'Gifts for the good; birch for the bad. That's how it's supposed to be on St. Nicholas' Day,' said Nigel's father. 'But at Christmas – now that's quite different. Everyone, good or bad, gets presents then.'

'So they do,' Nigel exclaimed. 'I wonder why.'

'Nigel,' said his mother, pretending to be very shocked 'Surely you know why? When God gave us Jesus, he didn't wait for us to be good first, did he?'

34

One of Us

SPRINGTIME – and Christmas. They seemed so different, so far apart. Certainly Graham would never have thought one would remind him of the other. But that is in fact what happened.

Christmas cards arriving thick and fast. Every morning there was a loud 'plop' at the front door as the postman pushed another batch through.

Graham enjoyed looking at them after his mother had arranged them in various parts of the house. But he was interested most of all in the ones that came from overseas. His father's business took him into many different countries; everywhere he went he made friends and many of them sent cards at Christmas.

One group of cards in particular made Graham stand and stare at them. Their subject was much the same – Mary with the child Jesus in her arms. Yet in one respect they were quite different.

There were six of them, from India, China, Africa, Italy, from Canada on the border of Eskimo country, and one from a friend in England. Something about them puzzled him.

'Mum,' he called out. 'Come and look.' In a moment his mother joined him.

'See these cards?' he said, pointing to the five which had come from overseas. 'They're wrong.'

'In what way?' his mother asked.

'Look at the baby. One's brown, another is yellow; that one's black, the next looks a sort of olive colour. And *that* one,' he exclaimed, pointing to the card from Canada, 'he looks like a little Eskimo.'

'And what should they look like?'

'That one, of course,' Graham pointed to the card which

115

had come from one of their English friends. His mother paused for a moment.

'Graham, where was Jesus born?'

Looking puzzled, Graham exclaimed, 'Bethlehem, Mother. We all know that.'

'Whereabouts is that?'

'Palestine, of course.'

His mother pointed to the English card.

'And you think Jesus looked like that when he was born?'

Graham stared at the cards again. 'No, of course, he wouldn't. He was a Jewish baby, born in Palestine.' His face fell again. 'So they're *all* wrong. Ours looks English, the Indian looks Indian and . . .'

'I don't think they're so wrong,' his mother said. 'What those cards show is this. Wherever Christians celebrate the birth of Jesus, they think of him as just like them, one of themselves. You see . . .'

Graham's mother went on speaking and then suddenly stopped.

'Graham, I don't believe you're hearing a word I'm saying. You seem miles away.'

She was quite right. He was. And thinking of something that happened many months before, in the Spring.

Uncle Jim used to take him out for the day to all sorts of places. He was the sort of person who seems to notice things other people miss. Often he would suggest going to one of the 'stately homes', or an old church, or just for a walk in the woods. It would sound a bit dull in advance. But not when the time came; not when you went with Uncle Jim. He made everything so interesting.

One day, after they had visited an old church in the heart of the country, they were standing outside and Uncle Jim was pointing out several interesting things. Suddenly, from around the ancient porch came a great commotion and fluttering of birds' wings.

'Whatever are they making all that fuss about?' said Graham.

'I expect there's a nest in that porch. Not many people disturb them, I fancy. They're afraid we shall disturb their new family.'

Graham started to call out to the excited birds. 'It's all right. Don't panic. We won't hurt you.' And he made some poor imitations of bird sounds.

'It's no good, my boy,' said Uncle Jim. 'They don't understand you. You are probably making them more bothered than ever.'

'I wish I could make them understand,' Graham exclaimed.

'Well now, there's only one way you could do that.'

'How? Tell me.'

'You would have to become a bird yourself, just like them, one of themselves. By the way,' his Uncle had added, 'you might think about that at Christmas-time.'

Graham had no idea what Uncle Jim meant; not then.

But now, as he stood looking at the Christmas cards, each one picturing the baby Jesus, and heard his mother's words, Graham thought perhaps he *did* understand.

'They think of Jesus as just like them, one of themselves . . .' she had said. He turned to her. 'I suppose, really, that was the only way he could make us understand what he had to tell us,' he said, 'by becoming one of us. It's rather like me and the birds,' he added, and laughed when his mother looked very puzzled. 'Uncle Jim will know what I mean.'

35

Decorating for Christmas

CEDRIC and his friends watched the other boys and girls of the village gathering greenery for the Festival of Light. They wished they could join in. But they knew it would be no good. If they went home carrying bundles of holly and ivy, laurel and mistletoe, they would only be told to throw them away.

One of the village boys came up to the group. 'Poor old Christians,' he taunted. 'Haven't got any greenery. Here, take some of mine.' He thrust a bundle of ivy towards Cedric.

'No thank you,' said Cedric.

'No thank you,' imitated the boy. 'You mean you daren't. Come on, I dare you. Take it home.'

'I said, No,' repeated Cedric.

'Why not?' demanded the boy. 'You always used to have it. Why can't you now, now that you have – what do you call it? – Christmas?'

'I don't really understand,' stammered Cedric. 'We only know we mustn't.'

It was midwinter in Saxon England many centuries ago. Each year, as the days began to lengthen once more, everyone was winning the victory over winter darkness. So they kept what they called the Festival of Light. There was feasting and fun, presents were exchanged, ordinary work ceased, and homes were decorated with extra lamps – and with greenery.

Among the Saxons the people who became Christians grew in number. At this time of the year they, too, had a Festival to keep. They remembered the birth of Jesus.

At first, they thought they would have a quite separate one of their own, not connected with the Festival of Light. But they changed their minds.

'It seems a pity to have two festivals,' said their leaders. 'After all, we are as glad as anyone that the light is coming back again. And is not Jesus the Light of the World?'

'So what we have decided is this,' declared the chief Christian. 'We will keep the Festival of Light as our neighbours do. But,' and he paused to be sure everyone was listening, 'for us it will mean much more. For us it will be Christ-mass, the Feast of Christ, the Light of the World.'

And that is what they did. They had family fun and feasting, but remembered most of all the family in Bethlehem – Mary, Joseph and their newly born child. They gave one another presents, but also thought of the gifts brought to the Manger.

Everything was just the same as in their neighbours' homes who kept only the Festival of Light. Everything – except the decorations, the holly and the ivy, the laurel and the mistletoe. They were forbidden, because, their leaders said, all of them were linked with heathen worship. No Christian home should have such things.

Then, gradually, things began to change. One by one Christian homes included greenery in their decorations. Word soon got round. The Christian leaders were angry. They called a meeting.

'We have a rule forbidding greenery because it is used in heathen worship. That rule is being broken. We demand to know why.'

A man named Boniface stood up and spoke. 'With respect, sir, some of us think the ban is unnecessary. Take the laurel, for instance.'

'The laurel is sacred to Apollo, a Greek so-called god,' snapped a leader. 'But perhaps you did not know that.'

'Is that so?' replied Boniface, quite undisturbed. 'I will tell you what it speaks to me about. Victory. Everyone knows a laurel wreath is the winner's prize. Jesus has won the victory for us over darkness and evil.'

Even the older men who had been against the whole idea had to nod their heads slowly in agreement.

'What about the holly?' they asked. 'You know that our ancestors have used it in their pagan worship for as long as anyone can remember.'

In answer, a man stepped forward holding some holly branches in his hand. As the people watched he interweaved a number of them into a circle.

'Does this put you in mind of anything?' he inquired. They shook their heads.

The man then raised the holly wreath and placed it, very carefully, on his head. He saw the watchers stir, though they said nothing.

'I put this on my head very gently,' he said. 'Suppose I had rammed it on, hard. Can you see what would have happened? The prickly spikes would have pierced my skin and made it bleed. Red blood, red as those berries the holly bears.'

There was a moment of complete silence. Then an old woman murmured quietly,

'The crown of thorns. The drops of blood on the Saviour's brow. The holly will remind us of him.'

But there were other decorations which were open to question. What, for example, about the mistletoe bough?

'You know very well that our ancestors, the Druids used it,' said the objectors. 'They thought it was a god and worshipped it.'

Some of the Christians looked uncomfortable. Perhaps the mistletoe ought to go – just to show their neighbours that they thought all this talk about its being a god was nonsense to any Christian. Then one of them spoke up quietly.

'There's a tale about mistletoe which my grandfather told, and his father before him, I believe. Two enemies met in a forest one winter's day. They quarrelled, then fought, till suddenly they looked up, and out of the tree beneath which they fought, they saw growing a mistletoe bough. Both stopped still. They could not fight in the presence of a god. That bough was a peace-maker.' He paused a moment. Then, firmly, he added. 'As far as my house is concerned, the mistletoe can stay. When I look at it, I'll remember the Prince of Peace.'

'And I, too, will have it,' said another man, stepping forward. It was Caedmon who was usually sent for when someone was ill; he had brought about many cures. 'It has given me a medicine which I have often used to heal the sick.' The people listened closely, for Caedmon was greatly respected.

'I care nothing for the Druids,' he went on, 'nor for their empty worship. No! When I see the mistletoe branch I shall remember Jesus – for he never failed to have compassion on the sick, and healed many.'

Finally the chief Christian stepped forward.

'Have it as you will then. Decorate your homes if you must. But not with ivy; not with that. Everyone knows that is the badge of Bacchus, god of wine. No pagan god shall have his badge in a Christian home.'

Even those who most wanted to decorate with greenery had to admit he seemed to be right. There was a general murmur of agreement. Then Chad the farmer spoke.

'I think we should delay a moment before we decide this,' he said quietly. Everyone thought a lot of Chad and they listened intently.

'In late autumn and into the winter, the birds are hard put to it to find shelter. But there is something which never fails them.'

He ran his hand over the walls of the barn round which they had gathered. He touched the green leaves of the plant which grew up it, spreading on each side.

'The ivy,' said Chad. 'There's shelter there, however hard the weather. And there's something else a few of you know. When the bees are short of the means to make honey because the flowers have faded, the ivy spreads out its leaves for them. You've noticed, maybe, the sticky surface of an ivy leaf late in the season? It's a good friend, is the ivy.'

'Bacchus,' he went on, 'who is he? He is not even real. Why should the friendly ivy remind me of him? No, my brother, I shall be thinking of the man they called a friend –

friend of tax-gatherers and sinners. Yes, I'll put up my ivy and remember him.'

So the Christians who wanted greenery won the day. Before the next Christmas, Cedric and his Christian friends joined the other boys and girls gathering greenery for the Festival of Light. They picked the ivy, and thought of Jesus, the friend. They gathered the laurel and were glad he was strong and victorious, they cut the holly and remembered the crown of thorns. They took the mistletoe bough home and thought of Jesus who made people well and brought peace.

If you could have gone into a Christian home or a pagan home in Saxon England in late December, they would have looked very much the same, with the people doing much the same things – eating and drinking, exchanging presents, celebrating.

But of course there was really a difference. For Cedric's family and their friends it was not just the Festival of Light. It was Christmas.

36

Three Wise Boys

ANDREW, Peter and Gordon lived in the same village, went to the same school, and the same church. They played together whenever they could, in fact, they were hardly ever seen apart.

On Saturdays and in holiday time they would go for long walks up the hills and through the woods and by the river. They climbed trees, looked for birds nests, went swimming, picked blackberries and nuts.

All the time, of course, they were getting older. Andrew was the first to have his eleventh birthday. When Peter and Gordon came round to wish him a Happy Birthday, there stood his present from his Mum and Dad – a brand new gleaming bicycle. 'Just what I wanted,' he told his friends. You can imagine how envious they were, but each was allowed to have a go. Soon it was time for school.

After school Andrew went home to his cycle. Peter and Gordon went to their homes each with one thing in mind. As soon as their fathers came home the same question was asked, 'Dad, can I have a bicycle for my birthday?' 'You'll have to wait and see,' was the only reply they got. Sure enough, when their birthdays came round they each had a new bicycle. A policeman came to the school to show them how to make sure that their machines were safe. Each of the three friends was presented with a cycling proficiency flag (which meant they had passed their test) to be fastened on the front of his cycle. Now on Saturdays and in holidays they were often seen setting off on long cycle rides together.

It was getting near to Christmas and they began to talk of what they would do. Before they broke up from school their teacher talked to them about Christmas. She said that most people had good times with parties and presents, Christmas trees, crackers and all the rest. She went on to say that

Christmas meant something much more than all these things. Perhaps one day they would discover this meaning just as the three Wise Men did. They followed the star which led them to Jesus and they worshipped him.

The three friends were glad to be on holiday. They decided that if the next day was fine they would set out for a lovely long ride. The weather forecast was good so quite early they met. 'Where shall we go?' they all said together. Coming down the road they saw old Tom the Postman. He had a bag of letters almost too heavy for him to carry. They couldn't very well go off and leave him, so they offered to help. They ran from the gates up to the doors of the houses and very soon the bag grew lighter.

The three friends almost forgot their trip and, when they told old Tom about it, he suggested they should cycle over to the Lake at Puddleton and see if they could find out how Harry the ferryman was who lived on the island. He had one or two boats which he used to row people over to the island and he was a fisherman as well. Tom the Postman hadn't seen or heard anything of Harry for some time.

Off the three boys set – a good ten miles ride. There by the side of the lake was a boat moored. On a post there was a bell with a notice which said, 'Ring bell for ferry'. Peter rang the bell hard and they waited, but there was no sign of Harry.

They decided to row over to the island and see if anything was the matter. They scrambled into the boat. Andrew took one oar and Gordon the other. Peter steered. In about five minutes they had reached the island. They could see the little cottage where Harry lived and the little path leading up to it. There was no sign of life. 'Knock, knock', but no one answered. All they could hear was a faint groan. Gordon opened the door and there they saw old Harry sitting in his chair, obviously very ill. He was pleased to see them. They lit a fire and then made him a good hot drink.

Andrew said he would row back to the mainland and get a doctor. Peter and Gordon stayed and cleared up the cottage. Meanwhile, Andrew cycled to the village and telephoned for the doctor, promising to wait for him and row him over to the island.

The doctor declared that Harry was too ill to stay there and said he would get him into hospital. 'Could you boys stay here until the ambulance comes?' They agreed to do that.

Again Andrew rowed the boat back and waited for the ambulance. Before long he heard the siren and the ambulance men had lots of warm blankets and hot water bottles which they took over to the island.

Old Harry was soon wrapped up and carried to the boat and before long he was tucked up in bed in hospital. The boys were allowed to visit him. The Ward was beautifully decorated for Christmas. There was a large Christmas tree in the corner.

The next Sunday there was a special Christmas Gift Service at church. The Minister said that gifts are not always things which we can see and feel but the greatest of all gifts is love and kindness. In our kindness to others we are worshipping the one who was born at Christmas.

Andrew, Peter and Gordon looked at each other and smiled. When they sang the last hymn, they realized something of the real meaning of Christmas; 'Love came down at Christmas'.